AF576617

THE CROSS AND BEYOND

THE CROSS AND BEYOND

ROY E. DE BRAND

BROADMAN PRESS
Nashville, Tennessee

© Copyright 1983 • Broadman Press

All rights reserved

4222-50

ISBN: 0-8054-2250-1

Dewey Decimal Classification: 232.96

Subject Headings: JESUS CHRIST—CRUCIFIXION—SERMONS //
JESUS CHRIST—RESURRECTION—SERMONS

Library of Congress Catalog Card Number: 83-70374

Printed in the United States of America

Unless otherwise noted, Scripture quotations are from the Revised Standard Version of the Bible, copyrighted 1946, 1952, © 1971, 1973.

Scripture quotations marked (KJV) are from the King James Version of the Bible.

Scripture quotations marked (NIV) are from the HOLY BIBLE *New International Version,* copyright © 1978, New York Bible Society. Used by permission.

Scripture quotations marked (TLB) are from *The Living Bible.* Copyright © Tyndale House Publishers, Wheaton, Illinois, 1971. Used by permission.

Library of Congress Cataloging in Publication Data
De Brand, Roy E.
The cross and beyond.

1. Easter—Sermons. 2. Jesus Christ—Passion—
Sermons. 3. Sermons, American. I. Title.
BV4259.D4 1984 252'.62 83-70374
ISBN 0-8054-2250-1 (pbk.)

To my mother
and in memory of my father
who led me to the cross
and taught me to live
in the light of the open tomb.

Preface

The cross, resurrection, and post-resurrection narratives of the New Testament form the central focus of the Christian faith. Everything before these events points to them. Everything since looks back on them. This book is an attempt to look deeply into those events as they might have been experienced had we been there. Would we have been among the jeering multitudes, the sneering scribes, or the cheering followers? There's really no way to say. But perhaps a venture into the narratives can help us understand the people who were there better and more clearly define where we are today in relationship to Christ.

The chapters comprising this book were originally sermons delivered from the pulpit of the First Baptist Church of Americus, Georgia. Section I was a preparatory series leading up to Easter. I thought that by looking at people around the cross, then hearing the seven sayings of Jesus from the cross, we might better understand its significance. My people were very receptive to these messages and encouraging toward their publication. Included in these messages is some of my poetry. If the author isn't otherwise identified, I wrote the poetry.

You will easily recognize Section II as Easter messages. The resurrection evokes more awe and confirms our unique faith more than any other single event. If not for the resurrection, the cross would lose its significance. So from each of the four Gospel narratives, the messages sprang which I hope will lead each reader to an individual experience of the Easter faith. Would to God I could have been there! Maybe by these words we can each be led to understand the resurrection better, experience it more fully.

Section III deals with the events after the resurrection. Strange, but somehow we too often stop with Easter. A definite choice was made by those of Jesus' day about what they believed concerning the resurrection. The same choice is ours to make. And after it's made, we who follow must hear Jesus' final words of command and challenge. I hope these messages will help you to hear clearer and respond more positively.

To the good people of Americus who respond so enthusiastically to my preaching I owe a debt of gratitude. They make preaching rewarding and challenging.

To my wife, Carolyn, I owe most everything, not the least of which is much inspiration in the writing of this book and her typing of it. She's a blessing to all who know her. Especially to me.

I hope these messages transport your mind and heart to the cross, the resurrection, and its aftermath. We each need to go there. From there we need to go on into commitment to the One who died, rose again, and calls for our faith and service. I hope each of these chapters confronts you with the eternal question, "Were you there?"

ROY E. DE BRAND

Contents

Easter PM

Section I

Were You There . . . At the Cross?

1
Were You There . . . In Self-Righteousness?
Matthew 26:57-68

The plaintive old spiritual asks, "Were you there when they crucified my Lord?" The priests and scribes and elders were there. They stood steeped in self-righteousness as the Savior was sentenced to die.

Who were these priests and scribes and elders? They were the rulers of the house of Israel; and they ruled so well that even when God sent his own Son, he couldn't get in! He was shut out by the self-righteousness of the religious establishment.

Some of these religious rulers were Pharisees. The word means "separated ones." In life they were totally separated to preserving the purity of the law. But they were coldly detached as the law was set aside to condemn Jesus.

Others were Sadducees—sneering socialites practicing politics to condemn God's Son, whose only crimes were service and selflessness.

Some were scribes. These professional interpreters of the law were, in reality, loveless legalists who hounded Jesus with technicalities during the years of his public ministry and held him up to ridicule during the hours of his personal misery on the cross.

Together these groups formed the Sanhedrin, the "supreme court" of Judaism. They connived against and condemned the supreme Son of God. They were there at the illegal trial preceding the crucifixion. They were there in pride and pomposity. In their self-righteousness, these religious rulers condemned Jesus.

Matthew says:

> Those who had arrested Jesus took him to Caiaphas, the high priest, where the teachers of the law and the elders had assembled. But Peter followed him at a distance, right up to the courtyard of the high priest. He entered and sat down with the guards to see the outcome.
>
> The chief priests and the whole Sanhedrin were looking for false evidence against Jesus so that they could put him to death. But they did not find any, though many false witnesses came forward.
>
> Finally two came forward and declared, "This fellow said, 'I am able to destroy the temple of God and rebuild it in three days.'"
>
> Then the high priest stood up and said to Jesus, "Are you not going to answer? What is this testimony that these men are bringing against you?" But Jesus remained silent.
>
> The high priest said to him, "I charge you under oath by the living God: Tell us if you are the Christ, the Son of God."
>
> "Yes, it is as you say," Jesus replied. "But I say to all of you: In the future you will see the Son of Man sitting at the right hand of the Mighty One and coming on the clouds of heaven."
>
> Then the high priest tore his clothes and said, "He has spoken blasphemy! Why do we need any more witnesses? Look, now you have heard the blasphemy. What do you think?"
>
> "He is worthy of death," they answered.
>
> Then they spit in his face and struck him with their fists. Others slapped him and said, "Prophesy to us, Christ. Who hit you?" (26:57-68, NIV).

They were there, these scribes and Pharisees, robed in their self-righteousness, condemning the Son of God. And we need to examine ourselves to see if our self-righteousness condemns him yet today. We are at the cross of Christ when we stand in self-righteousness and condemn the Son of God. How does this happen? How do we become so self-righteous that we crucify the Son of righteousness?

Self-Righteous Creedalism

First, we become self-righteous when we absolutize our faith into creeds. That's what happened to the priests, scribes, and elders. Their once living faith became a concrete creed and died by asphyxiation.

Jesus came to bring life and light. The self-righteous scribes and polarized Pharisees practiced lifeless legalism to the point their eyes were blinded to God's Light. Grace and Truth came and walked among them. But they didn't know because they'd painted themselves into the corner of creedalism at the dead-end street of self-righteousness.

"I charge you under oath by the living God: Tell us if you are the Christ, the Son of God," shouted the high priest. If they hadn't been so steeped in self-righteousness, they would not have needed such a statement from Christ. But they were so preoccupied with their Pharisaism and so self-satisfied with the status quo that, even when Jesus told them yes he was the Son of God, they simply retreated into the comfort of their creed and condemned Jesus. He didn't fit into their contrived creed, so he had to go.

One day I was looking at a home computer in an electronics store. The salesman had praised all the virtues of a particular model, hoping to sell it to me. He was hoping against hope. A computer wizard I am not! But I listened politely as he explained various functions to me. Then he asked me to try it out. I punched in what I thought was proper data. Then I punched the button calling for a response. On the screen flashed the ominous words, "Data doesn't compute!"

The same response is evoked when you try to enter the

living Lord into a closed creedal religion. He didn't "compute" with the scribes and Pharisees, just as he won't fit into any prescribed human-made religion with all the pat answers based on what we do rather than what God's done for us!

Don't crowd Christ out of your faith by confining him to a narrow system. The abundant life can't be contained in a creed. To try to do so is to repeat the sin of the scribes and priests and elders. It's the sin of self-righteousness that absolutizes faith into creeds. Christ won't penetrate that shell of self-righteousness. Keep your faith alive and open to the living Christ!

The Attitude of Condemnation

Then, too, we become self-righteous when we adopt the attitude of condemnation. Jesus was a disturber of the status quo. He didn't fit into the theology of the priests and scribes and elders, so they schemed to get rid of him. They developed the attitude of condemnation. It reached its peak at the midnight trial of Jesus. When he announced himself as the Christ, the Messiah, God's Son, he needed say no more. He was condemned already in their minds. Listen to the reaction to Jesus' claim. "The high priest tore his clothes . . . 'He has spoken blasphemy! Why do we need any more witnesses? . . . What do you think?'" And they all adopted the same condemnatory attitude: "He is worthy of death."

The religious rulers at Jesus' trial had convinced themselves they were God's people. They were doing God's work; no one else was. It's only a short step from such self-righteousness to becoming convinced everything you do is justified. Then the attitude of condemnation develops and everything, everyone, else is judged by it. Anything or anyone who doesn't fit the self-standard mold stands condemned. Jesus was a victim of the attitude of condemnation.

The scribes and Pharisees aren't the only people in history to develop the attitude of condemnation. Such an attitude gave us the Crusades in the eleventh century in which Europe was swept with slaughtering for the cross. Thousands died as a result!

The same attitude brought about the Inquisition, beginning at the close of the thirteenth century, leading to the torture and execution of dissidents in the name of religious orthodoxy.

It was the attitude of condemnation that caused the witch hunts in the late seventeenth and early eighteenth centuries in England, Scotland, and especially Salem, Massachusetts. Yes, even in America, fifty-five people were tortured and twenty were executed because of religious superstition and the self-righteous attitude of condemnation.

Lest we be too quick to judge those of the past who held this attitude of condemnation, let us examine our own. To be comfortable and secure in our faith is one thing. To point others to Christ is our task. But to condemn and villify others because they don't believe like we do is a sin. Indeed, it's a part of the sin of the scribes and Pharisees that put Jesus on the cross. Were you there?

The proper attitude must be, "Lord I believe; help thou mine unbelief" (Mark 9:24, KJV). Too often it's, "Lord, I believe; help their unbelief!"

When the self-righteous rule, watch out for the attitude of condemnation!

The Action of Crucifixion

Ultimately we become self-righteous when we employ the action of crucifixion. It's a short step from attitude to action. When both are based on the presumption that we are right and everyone else is wrong, the landscape easily becomes dotted with crosses!

So it was with Jesus before the high court. The attitude became the action. They proclaimed him deserving of death. "Then they spit in his face and struck him with their fists." Others slapped him and said, "Prophesy to us, Christ. Who hit you?"

These same people would, in a few hours, demand the crucifixion of Jesus. The ultimate act of self-righteousness is the elimination of all that threatens the security of the self!

For the scribes, elders, and priests it was the elimination of Jesus. For Adolf Hitler it was the elimination of Jews, Communists, Poles, Czechs, and others. Martin Niemoller was a Lutheran pastor in Germany when Hitler came to power. He said, "When Hitler's henchmen came to arrest the Communists, I was not a Communist, so I didn't speak up. Then they came for the Jews. I was not a Jew so I didn't speak up. They came for the Trade Unionists and I was not a member, so I was silent. They came for the Catholics, and I was a Protestant, so I didn't speak up. Then they came for me and by that time no one was left to speak up."

By the time beliefs become creeds and condemnatory attitudes develop, it's getting late to stop the actions of elimination. Jesus became their victim.

So the place to start is with a vibrant, living faith leading to openness in attitude toward others and actions of love and selfless service. Anything less is unchristian and anything else is unhealthy.

Were you there when they crucified my Lord? We were and are anytime our beliefs fossilize into uncaring creeds. We stand steeped in self-righteousness whenever our attitudes condemn others by prejudice. We are there anytime our actions convey cruelty of any kind. We are there when we draw up our robes of self-righteousness around us and separate ourselves from caring, feeling, serving, seeing.

Every time we exercise self-righteousness, we hit the nail on the head in the hand of our Lord!

Were you there? We were and are whenever self-righteousness interferes with God's righteousness in our lives or in the lives of others. Give your self-righteousness to God and let him forgive you and save you from sin and self. Dedicate your life to fulfilling the righteousness of God. It far exceeds self-righteousness!

2
Were You There . . . Compelled to Christ?
Mark 15:21

Were you there when they crucified my Lord? Simon of Cyrene was, and he served the Savior with the strength of his shoulder. Only one verse in each of the three Synoptic Gospels tells us about Simon of Cyrene, and Mark 15:21 tells more than Matthew 27:32 or Luke 23:26. After Jesus' illegal trial, unfair condemnation, and torturous humiliation, the Romans put his cross on his back and led him out to crucify him. Then we read: "And they compelled a passerby, Simon of Cyrene, who was coming in from the country, the father of Alexander and Rufus, to carry his cross" (Mark 15:21, RSV).

We know of Simon the Cyrenian for only one reason. He was compelled to carry Jesus' cross. The Gospel of John tells us that Jesus bore his own cross; all condemned criminals did, but his strength gave out. The sham of a trial, the shameful scourging, the lack of sleep and food, and the weight of the world's sin all drained Jesus of his strength. As the macabre procession wound through the narrow streets of Jerusalem, taking the longest route possible as an example to other would-be criminals of the fate that might await them, Jesus stumbled beneath the weight of the wooden cross.

Oh, the Roman soldiers wouldn't lift a finger to help, but they pointed a finger at Simon, a curious bystander in the curious crowd who was conscripted into service to carry Jesus' cross.

There seems to be no great, mysterious theological significance to Simon carrying Jesus' cross. A lot of interpreters allegorize some meaning into the incident. They talk of Simon's self-denial, his willingness to be used of the Lord, his extraordinary ability or strength. The plain truth is, Simon just happened to be there and was arbitrarily picked.

And the fact that there's no great significance to Simon's bearing Jesus' cross is what's so significant! It teaches us that God can use anyone compelled to Christ. Whether by force of faith or drawn by the dimensions of Jesus' love, God can use you if you will.

Compelled by the Cross

God can use us if we're compelled by the cross. Simon of Cyrene had no great desire to serve. He likely wasn't a volunteer. He wasn't there that day for that purpose. He was on his way into Jerusalem from the countryside, probably a Passover pilgrim, when he was singled out to carry the cross. It could just as easily have been someone else in the crowd. But it happened to Simon, probably a Jew from North Africa. He was the one forced into service by the Romans.

For whatever reason he was in Jerusalem, whatever Simon's plans were for his day or his lifetime, they abruptly changed when he was compelled, this passerby, to carry Christ's cross.

There's a sense in which each of us lives under the same compulsion; and in that sense, we were there with Simon when they crucified the Lord. The hymn writer got it right when he wrote,

> Must Jesus bear the cross alone,
> And all the world go free?
> No, there's a cross for ev'ryone,
> And there's a cross for me.

That's what Jesus meant when he said, "If any man would come after me, let him deny himself and take up his cross daily and follow me" (Luke 9:23).

Were you there? When I read about Simon of Cyrene, compelled to carry the cross of Christ, I wish I had been him. Oh, to do that for Jesus!

Then, I hear him say, "Deny self, take up your cross daily." And I realize we are there. We are to be faithful unto death each day of life. We are to live in continual, sacrificial relationship with Jesus Christ. And in that sense, we're compelled to carry his cross. The only way God can use us is if we're willing, compelled to bear the cross.

Converted to Christ

God can use us if we're converted to Christ. Why is this incident of Simon in Scripture? If there's no great theological significance or hidden message in it, if just about anyone could have been compelled to carry Christ's cross and Simon just happened to be the one, why consider it at all? Because Simon of Cyrene was converted to faith in Jesus Christ as a result of being compelled to carry Jesus' cross. I'm fully convinced of this.

Surely Simon stayed to witness the outcome of the man whose cross he'd carried. How could anyone have walked away? Simon stayed. He saw the nails driven, heard the cross bump rudely into its socket. Simon heard Jesus say:

> "Father, forgive them."
> "To-day, shalt thou be with me in paradise."
> "Take care of my mother."
> "My God, my God, why?"
> "I thirst"
> "It is finished"
> "Father, into thy hands . . . "

And the compound experience of carrying Christ's cross

and watching him die on it drew Simon to believe in Jesus as Savior.

The very fact that we know Simon's name, hometown, and sons' names is mute testimony to his conversion. How do we know these facts? There were no reporters at Calvary, no television cameras, no post-crucifixion interviews. It stands to reason that we know Simon's name and city of origin and sons' names because they became participants in the early church. I think the simple truth of this story is that Simon was there, compelled to carry the cross, and was converted by its power.

Jesus said, "And I, if I be lifted up . . . will draw all men unto me" (John 12:32). The cross is the power of God unto salvation!

Were you there? You were and are if you know the saving grace of God through Christ's sacrifice on the cross. He died for your sins. By faith you can receive his gift of life and stand in the light of God's love that radiates from the cross. Let the compelling, converting power of the cross call you to faith in Christ. Confess him as Savior. Accept him as Lord. Let the power of the cross call you to discipleship. Join the followers of the cross in serving the Christ of the cross. Stand beneath the cross of Jesus, compelled and converted. You, too, can know the magnetism of his divine love!

3
Were You There . . . Crying Out to Christ?
Luke 23:32-33,39-43

Were you there when they crucified my Lord? Two criminals were, and they each cried out to Christ with differing results. Luke 23:32-33,39-43 tells us about the criminals and their crying out to Christ:

> Two other men, both criminals, were also led out with him to be executed. When they came to the place called The Skull, there they crucified him, along with the criminals—one on his right, the other on his left.
>
> One of the criminals who hung there hurled insults at him: "Aren't you the Christ? Save yourself and us!"
>
> But the other criminal rebuked him. "Don't you fear God," he said, "since you are under the same sentence? We are punished justly, for we are getting what our deeds deserve. But this man has done nothing wrong."
>
> Then he said, "Jesus, remember me when you come into your kingdom."
>
> Jesus answered him, "I tell you the truth, today you will be with me in paradise" (NIV).

There were three crosses on Calvary the day Jesus died. He hung on the center cross. On each side of him hung a criminal, probably zealous Jewish insurgents, religious revolutionaries against the rigors of Roman rule. Each of these insurrectionists pled for life, but with entirely different motives. Each cried out to Christ for his own reasons, and the result for each was different.

On the middle cross was the Christ, the Messiah, the

Savior, Redeemer of all humanity. He died willingly, forgivingly. He was the only sinless person who ever lived. The dying criminals' response to this man on the center cross determined their destiny.

It's important for us to know what response they made to Christ and why and how they made it, for our response to Christ's sacrificial death determines our destiny. Were you there? Consider the responses of the two who cried out to Christ on the day they died with him.

The Cry of Separation

The cry from the first cross depicts separation. Tradition names the unrepentant thief Gestas. His crimes were political. He was dying that day for revolutionary acts against Rome. His response to Jesus on the center cross was to cry out, "Save yourself and us!"

This was no plea for the salvation of his soul. It was a desperate appeal for relief from the rigors of death by crucifixion. He saw only his temporal needs and pled for physical salvation. He cried out in utter selfishness.

He didn't acknowledge Jesus as the Christ. "Aren't you the Christ?" he cried. Or, as the King James Version has it, "If thou be Christ." There is every reason to believe it was a cry of derision; no faith there; no penitence; only self-centered sympathy seeking salvation from physical suffering.

He reaped only separation. He received only Jesus' silence. The dying Christ who had pled forgiveness for those who nailed him to the cross answered not a word to the unrepentant revolutionary. Gestas died alone, wanting all, giving nothing. He cried out to Christ only for what he could give and do for him. And his selfishness brought separation for all eternity. He was so near salvation, yet totally separated, forever!

Once when I was a boy I went into a five and dime store

with my mother. The store was crowded. She cautioned me to hold onto her hand tightly. But the allurement of dime store toys was too great a temptation. I struggled loose from her grip. After a few moments dawdling at the counter, I reached up and retook my mother's hand. Imagine my surprise when a strange voice said, "What you doin', Boy?" It wasn't my mother's hand!

The experience was frightening. For a moment I was scared speechless, lost, separated. I remember the fright to this day. I began to cry. Oh, what a relief it was when my mother came into view around the corner of the counter and reclaimed me!

Separation is a lonely, painful feeling. The tragic consequence of dying without Jesus Christ as your Savior is eternal separation from God. The most chilling, tragic truth about the cross, seen in the unrepentant criminal, is that it's possible to be there and still miss its saving effect! It's possible to know all about Jesus' dying love and not accept it, not believe in him, not become a part of his kingdom.

It's up to you. Not to believe brings separation.

The Cry of Salvation

The cry from the second cross depicts salvation received. Dismas is the name tradition gives the penitent criminal. His is the only "deathbed conversion" in the New Testament. He cried out to Christ and received salvation.

Dismas rebuked his companion in crime. He asked, "Don't you fear God?" Dismas did. It was obvious in his own confession of sin. "We are punished justly," he exclaimed. It was an acknowledgment of his sinfulness. But he detected the sinless character of the man on the center cross, "But this man has done nothing wrong!" In his humility, he was a stark contrast to his comrade-in-arms who cried out only in selfishness.

Then the most amazing thing happened. Above the din of the crowd, the rude ridicule directed at Jesus by the religious rulers, the gambling, mocking soldiers' smugness, there came a cry of faith and a confession of Christ that rang the bells of heaven! "Jesus, remember me when you come into your kingdom." Instead of Jesus the victim hanging on the cross beside him, Dismas saw the Christ of salvation! He believed and cried out in faith.

His faith was rewarded on the spot. Jesus' kingdom had come and Dismas would be a part of it. "Today you will be with me in paradise," Jesus answered him. To his surprise, Dismas received immediate salvation. His cry of faith was rewarded with the certainty of salvation!

Do you remember when you received Christ? It was the same way. You saw your need, believed in Christ, asked for him to save you, and you received salvation right then, right there. And if you haven't done that yet, you can come to Christ the same way. Were you there? Yes, all who receive Christ were there because we all come the same way—need, faith, confession, repentance, salvation received. All who cry out to Christ, believing, receive salvation.

The Savior We Cry Out To

The third cross depicts the Savior we must cry out to. He is revealed in a unique way in this passage. We see him clearly as the Savior. He is able to "save them to the uttermost that come unto God by him" (Heb. 7:25). We see that here. The cross was a necessary step in that process of salvation. The cross provided the power to save. He died that we might know life. Our redemption was his achievement, and the cross was the means.

Jesus alone held the keys to the kingdom. He opened the door for Dismas. He opens it for all who believe.

The cross reveals Jesus' love. No one who cries out to

him in faith will be forsaken. No matter how black the heart or how late the hour, Jesus saves those who repent and believe. He does it because he loves. Love was his only motivation for the cross. It was a great sacrifice made with great love.

All great world religions offer salvation by some means. Some propose escape into some all-absorbing universal mind as the way. Others demand strict adherence to rules and regulations. A few propose thinking or philosophy as the way to God. Most advocate good works or goodwill to others, a sort of reward system based on what you do.

Only Christianity has a cross! It's God's way of salvation for us. The message of the cross is clear—sin must be paid for. Salvation comes not by what we do but by what's already been done for us. Jesus came, lived, loved, died, and rose again. That's the way of salvation! The only way, ever, for anyone.

Were you there when they crucified my Lord? Had you been present at Calvary on the day Jesus died, how would you have reacted to him? To reject him results in separation. To receive him results in salvation. He died for you. The choice is still yours. Cry out in faith and you can receive his forgiveness. Your response to Christ's sacrificial death determines your destiny.

4
Were You There . . . In Secret?
John 19:38-42

Were you there when they crucified my Lord? Joseph of Arimathea and Nicodemus were, and they watched in shocked silence as the Savior suffered and died. They had followed him from afar in fear. But when he was dead, Joseph of Arimathea and Nicodemus buried Jesus. The Gospel of John tells us about it. Jesus had died, and then:

> After this Joseph of Arimathea, who was a disciple of Jesus, but secretly, for fear of the Jews, asked Pilate that he might take away the body of Jesus, and Pilate gave him leave. So he came and took away his body. Nicodemus also, who had at first come to him by night, came bringing a mixture of myrrh and aloes, about a hundred pounds' weight. They took the body of Jesus, and bound it in linen cloths with the spices, as is the burial custom of the Jews. Now in the place where he was crucified there was a garden, and in the garden a new tomb where no one had ever been laid. So because of the Jewish day of Preparation, as the tomb was close at hand, they laid Jesus there (19:38-42).

Actually all four Gospels tell about the burial of Jesus, and we have to put all four together to get a complete picture. Matthew and Mark add the detail that the burial was at evening. Mark explains that it was the day of preparation, the day before the sabbath, in other words, Friday evening. Luke tells us Arimathea was a Jewish settlement, Joseph's home. Both Matthew and John let us know Joseph was a disciple of Jesus, but John alone adds, "but secretly, for fear of the Jews."

Joseph of Arimathea had reason to be fearful. The Sanhedrin had seen to it that Jesus was crucified. Mark indicates Joseph was a member of that council, and we already know Nicodemus was too. Luke not only tells us that Joseph had not consented in the decision of that high court to condemn Jesus but also assesses Joseph's character as a "good and righteous man" (23:50, RSV).

Mark says Joseph was "looking for the kingdom of God." Watching Jesus die, he surely found it! So Mark explains that Joseph "took courage" (15:43), (and it must have taken a great deal) and went to Pilate and asked for Jesus' body. Pilate wondered if Jesus were already dead, and the centurion confirmed it, Mark adds. Matthew tells us Jesus' body was wrapped in a clean linen shroud. Mark says it was laid in a rock-hewn tomb, and Luke adds the detail that the tomb was previously unused.

John alone indicates that Nicodemus was a partner with Joseph in Jesus' burial. He brought burial spices, this same religious ruler who came to Jesus by night and heard him say "Ye must be born again" (3:7, KJV).

Matthew says two Marys sat by the tomb. Mark says they saw where he was laid. Luke adds that they saw how he was laid, and John locates the tomb in a garden near the cross.

When you read the four Gospel accounts of the burial of Jesus, with all the details, it has the "ring of truth" J. B. Phillips wrote about. There's no doubt about the facts that Jesus died and was buried nor about the circumstances and people involved.

But there are some questions we'd like to ask Joseph of Arimathea and Nicodemus. Why were they secret disciples? What made them come out openly after Jesus was dead?

As we examine ourselves in relation to Jesus, we must

ask ourselves, Had I been there, would it have been in secret? And what kind of disciple of Jesus am I today? Were you there in secret? Let's examine this question by first looking at some reasons for secret discipleship.

Reasons for Secret Discipleship

It's intriguing that John identifies Joseph of Arimathea as a secret disciple of Jesus. What is secret discipleship? Nicodemus obviously was in the same category. They weren't open, practicing disciples of Jesus during his brief, three-year public ministry, as were Matthew, Simon Peter, Andrew, James, John, and the rest of the twelve apostles. Even Simon Peter concealed his discipleship when it was expedient to do so! Why secret discipleship?

For one thing, Joseph and Nicodemus had too much fear. They feared losing status as respected religious and community leaders. They feared losing their position on the "supreme court" of Judaism, the Sanhedrin. They feared losing money, as many did who gave up everything to follow Jesus. And most of all, they feared for their very lives. Had they followed Jesus openly, they could just as easily have been beside him on crosses that day. Fear consumed them and prevented active, open discipleship.

They also had too little faith. They wanted to believe Jesus was who he said he was and could do what he said he could. Joseph was "looking for the kingdom," as Mark puts it. And Nicodemus had heard the necessary faith relationship explained clearly by Jesus himself when he went to him by night. He knew he had to be born from above! They wanted to believe. It just took the cross to fully convince them.

And they had too few facts. In life Joseph and Nicodemus were seekers, questioners, pilgrims. But in seeing Jesus die, in hearing what he said while dying—only in his death did they finally become finders, committed to him.

There are far too many secret disciples today! Great numbers of would-be followers have too much fear, too little faith, and too few facts and therefore commitment to Christ is questionable. Are you one of those? Where do you stand? What do you believe? To whom are you committed?

William Barclay says, "There is no such thing as a 'secret' disciple. For either the discipleship will destroy the secrecy or the secrecy will destroy the discipleship."

Joseph of Arimathea and Nicodemus couldn't stand seeing their Lord die, so their discipleship destroyed their secrecy. They "took courage," expressed their faith, finalized their commitment, went to Pilate, and asked for the body of Jesus and buried him. Maybe you need to do the same. Go public with your discipleship and say, "I'm one of his and I'll live like it, talk like it, act like it, and let it make all the difference in my life from now on!"

This may mean a change in your life-style, a recommitment to Christ. It may call for identification with other disciples by church membership. Maybe it means for you professing Christ as your Savior and becoming a disciple. There's every reason in the world for open discipleship and not a single one for secret discipleship.

Let's look at some reasons for open discipleship.

Reasons for Open Discipleship

As you ponder the story of Jesus' burial and the role of Joseph of Arimathea and Nicodemus in it, try to analyze what it was that brought their discipleship into the open. Surely a part of it was Jesus' real death. He died. There could be no doubt of that. His death was agonizing, excruciating for Jesus and all who even leaned toward belief in him. And in Jesus' dying came the convincing revelation of his messiahship. Joseph and Nicodemus saw him die. They heard him speak seven times from the cross. And their fears subsided, their faith was strengthened, and the facts were confirmed as Jesus died for them. They knew it, experienced it, and it opened up the way of discipleship for them.

Jesus' death gave them new life. They were "born from above." The new birth Nicodemus hadn't understood earlier he now experienced at the cross. Joseph did too. Life from death is what the cross is all about.

This new life gave them new courage. To go to Pilate and ask for Jesus' body was tantamount to a public acknowledgment of discipleship. In their newfound courage, they publicly identified with Jesus. They added to their new courage new generosity by the gift of the tomb. It was an offering of great generosity and personal sacrifice.

And what about you? Have you experienced the real death of Jesus, the fact that he died for your sin? Have you experienced the new life he gives by faith in him? When you do it will open the way for you to ask yourself, "What can I do for Jesus?" This question is answered in the poem, "What Jesus Needs."

> He doesn't need a crown,
> To put upon his brow;
> He had one once,
> But has another now.
>
> He doesn't need a cross,
> To carry up a hill;
> He had one once,
> But never again will.
>
> He doesn't need a tomb,
> To lay his body in;
> He had one once,
> But then he rose again.
>
> He only needs from you,
> Your faith and life and love;

That's all he needs,
To rejoice forever above!

Jesus needs from you an open declaration of faith, an open and obvious discipleship. Were you there? We were and are, but it must never be in secret!

What can you do for Jesus? Follow him—openly, committedly, now!

5
The Prayer That Gives Perspective
Luke 23:33-34

1|88

Had you been standing by the cross of Christ the six hours it took him to die you would have heard him speak seven times. The soldiers crucified Jesus at 9:00 AM. Instead of tying him to the cross, as they usually did in crucifixion, they nailed him to it. It was the ultimate in agony and insult. Then, they lifted the cross up, its base jolting rudely into its socket with a thud. You would have expected Jesus to first cry out in pain or agonize aloud, "Why me, why me?" Instead, his first words were a prayer.

I call Jesus' first words "The Prayer That Gives Perspective." They open up the whole realm of relationship to God. They help us see him more clearly. They show us our own needs.

Jesus' first saying on the cross is recorded in only one place in the Bible, Luke 23:33-34: "And when they came to the place which is called The Skull, there they crucified him, and the criminals, one on the right and one on the left. And Jesus said, 'Father, forgive them; for they know not what they do.'"

It would surprise no follower of Jesus that his first word while dying was a prayer. He was known by his praying in life. He would be recognized by prayer after the resurrection. In dying, he prayed. And this particular prayer gives a unique perspective to our knowledge of God, to the saving work of Jesus Christ, and to ourselves. Let's look at

"The Prayer That Gives Perspective."

Perspective on God

Jesus' first word from the cross is a prayer that gives a unique perspective on God. Jesus prayed, "Father." This tells us something about God. We know a lot about God. We know he is Creator, Righteous Judge, King of kings, Lord of the universe. But in his dying agony, Jesus didn't cry out, "O Creator of the world, forgive them!" He didn't say, "O King of the universe, forgive them!" His plea wasn't, "O Judge of their sins, forgive them!" But he cried, "Father, forgive them!"

This tells us that in all his roles and revelations, God's fatherhood is foremost. God is a concerned, caring, compassionate Father who loves us as his children. His love is clearly expressed in Jesus' first word from the cross—"Father."

How do you think of God? I once knew a young lady whose relationship to her abusive, drunken father was so terrible she couldn't conceive of a loving, caring Father God. She had to think of God in the feminine gender to have any faith at all!

How do you think of God? I've often wondered, if it had been my hands pierced by the nails and my body hanging on the cross, would I have done like Jesus and prayed, or would I have cursed God for putting me there? And the frightening thing is, I think I know!

How do you think of God? When life tumbles in, evil reigns triumphant, and you feel all alone, do you cry out to him as Father? What should you do?

Jesus provides the answer in his first word from the cross. You reaffirm faith in God as wise and loving Father who is in charge of your life, even in your darkest hours. It's a perspective from the cross on God that we need!

Perspective on Jesus

The first word from the cross also gives us a unique perspective on Jesus. It was not just a prayer. It was an intercessory prayer. Jesus prayed for his crucifiers, "Father, forgive them." Since every sin ever committed helped put Jesus on the cross, he prayed for us.

The theologians debate the subjects of Jesus' prayer. Was he asking forgiveness for the soldiers who'd nailed him there, the Pharisees who framed him, Pilate who could have spared him, Judas who betrayed him? All of these? None of these? I think I know. I believe it was for all of these and more that he prayed. This includes you and me. I believe Jesus asked God to forgive all sinners for all time. That was why he died.

His intercessory prayer was timeless and universal. It exemplifies the reason for which he came. Jesus came to forgive sin, to give love and life, to bring salvation, to make peace with God possible. It only became possible with Jesus' sacrificial death. So, as he died, he prayed for sinners. "Father, forgive them."

Perhaps of all spiritual disciplines, forgiveness is the easiest to receive and hardest to practice. First John 1:9 says, "If we confess our sins, he is faithful and just to forgive us our sins" (KJV). We believe this. We need it. But how much harder it is to forgive those who sin against us! Not the little, picky sins that fill our days, but the hard, major sins that plague our lives.

I read once of an Episcopal priest administering the Lord's Supper. One of his members came to the communion rail, knelt, and waited to be served. Before the priest could get to him, he got up and left. He walked to the rear of the church and stood. In a few moments he returned to the rail and received the bread and wine with tears in his eyes.

After the service the priest inquired about the incident. The man explained, "When I got to the rail I noticed the man beside me was my father's old boss. He drove my dad to an early grave. Bitterness and hatred welled up inside me, and I walked away. I couldn't receive communion. But when I got to the back of the sanctuary, I saw the stained glass window with the picture of Christ on the cross. As I looked at it, his words, "Father, forgive them, for they know not what they do," came into my mind. And I figured if he could forgive like that, so could I!"

Hear Jesus' word from the cross, "Father, forgive them." Receive that forgiveness. Practice it in the manner you have received it. That's why Jesus came. That's what he'd have you do.

Perspective on Self

The first word from the cross is a prayer that gives perspective on ourselves. Yes, we see God more clearly because of Jesus' prayer. Yes, we understand more fully Jesus' work of forgiveness. But the haunting phrase of his first saying is "for they know not what they do."

Who didn't know what they were doing? Pilate understood that he was crucifying an innocent man as he washed his hands of the whole affair. Judas was so conscious of his guilt as he sold both his soul and his Savior for thirty pieces of silver that he committed suicide. Annas and Caiaphas who calculated to drive this good man to his death knew what they were doing.

So what did Jesus mean when he prayed, "Father, forgive them; for they know not what they do?" Just this—he wasn't excusing their sin or even their abysmal ignorance. This was a plea to remove not only their spiritual blindness but ours as well.

It was a prayer of intercession for humanity's ignorance of the extent of evil rampant in our world. God sent his

Son—holy, innocent, blameless, and our sins crucified him. God used his sacrificial death to atone for our sins. Those who have not yet received his gift of salvation are ignorant still, "They know not what they do."

It's as if he prayed, "Forgive them, for they need forgiveness so desperately. Forgive them, for their sin is serious beyond their recognition." And all this was prayed in the name of the Father.

We need that kind of forgiveness, to that extent. Our condition without Christ is one of spiritual blindness and perpetual ignorance. If you let him come in, he'll open your eyes and illumine your mind.

The cross of Christ is an experience. Those who witnessed it were struck by its significance, as if by lightning. Let the lightning of Jesus' first saying from the cross strike into your experience. How we need this perspective on God as forgiving Father. How we need this perspective on Jesus' love. How we need this perspective on ourselves, both our inadequacy within ourselves and what we can be in Christ.

How do we get these perspectives? Stand beneath the cross of Jesus. Hear him pray, "Father, forgive them; for they know not what they do." Let it make the difference in you. Accept Christ. Dedicate your life to him. Follow him in discipleship and church membership. Let him have his way in your life and you too can know the perspective only he can give!

6
The Promise That Gives Paradise
Luke 23:39-43

Jesus' first saying from the cross as he hung dying was a prayer that gave perspective to the whole of theology. The second saying from the cross I call "The Promise That Gives Paradise." It, too, is recorded in only one place in the Bible, Luke 23:39-43:

> One of the criminals who were hanged railed at him, saying, "Are you not the Christ? Save yourself and us!" But the other rebuked him, saying, "Do you not fear God, since you are under the same sentence of condemnation? And we indeed justly; for we are receiving the due reward of our deeds; but this man has done nothing wrong." And he said, "Jesus, remember me when you come into your kingdom." And he said to him, "Truly, I say to you, today you will be with me in Paradise."

The first word was a prayer asking forgiveness. The second was an answer to a prayer, granting forgiveness. The first was an assurance of a blessed life. The second was an assurance of a blessed eternity. "Father, forgive them" shows Christ speaking to God on behalf of all people for all time. "Today you will be with me in Paradise," shows Christ speaking to an individual in a particular situation. How different the first two sayings from the cross! Let's examine the second saying, "The Promise That Gives Paradise."

Preceded by Repentance

Receiving the promise that gives paradise is preceded by repentance. We know little of the men who died alongside

Jesus. Luke described them using a word that means "common criminal." Others refer to them as thieves, insurrectionists, zealots. Tradition gives them names. The penitent thief is called Dismas. The unrepentant one is called Gestas. But that's about all we really know.

What we do know about them is they were being crucified. As they were dying, they joined the taunting crowd and mocking soldiers deriding Jesus. Matthew and Mark tell us this. But after three hours or so one of them had a change of heart. Dismas turned to Jesus in faith.

Gestas mocked on. "Are you not the Christ?" he baited, "Save yourself and us!" He would die disbelieving.

But Dismas mocked no more. He rebuked Gestas. "Do you not fear God?" Perhaps it was the way Jesus handled his suffering. Maybe it was the way Jesus looked at him. Surely Jesus' first words, "Father, forgive them" had made an impression on him. But in his dying moments a tiny flicker of faith fanned a flood of forgiveness and turned his slander to salvation.

It must always be that before there can be salvation there must first be repentance. The Old Testament prophesied it. John the Baptist proclaimed it. Jesus pronounced it so.

On March 9, 1981, twenty-four-year-old Stephen Judy died in Indiana's electric chair. He'd raped and murdered a young mother and drowned her three children. At a preexecution press conference, a reporter asked Judy if he was sorry for what he had done. He replied, "I don't lose no sleep over it!" He died unrepentant.

So did one of the insurgents on Calvary that day so long ago. But the other one repented. It didn't prolong his life, but it gave him life, spiritual life. Repentance is the only way to get it. It begins there.

If you would know life now you must turn away from your sins and to Jesus Christ. It's the only hope of heaven or promise of paradise you have.

Personal in Response

To receive the promise that gives paradise a personal response must be made to Christ. "Jesus, remember me!" Those words from the dying criminal brought the promise of paradise! It was a personal plea for pardon, a response to what he had seen and heard from Jesus. It wasn't much. He hadn't built a life of faith, but a life of rebellion and lawlessness. Only in those dying moments did he see another way. And what he saw he seized. What he beheld he believed. Though it wasn't much, it was enough, for we aren't saved by the abundance of our faith but by the superabundance of God's grace!

The two criminals were equidistant from Jesus. Each saw and heard what transpired in those hours. Both were wicked. Both suffered. Both were dying. Both needed forgiveness, salvation. Yet, one died in his sins and the other found forgiveness and a future with Christ. The difference was in their personal response to Jesus.

A man was witnessing to a friend about Jesus. His friend didn't want to be bothered at that moment. When pressed for a decision, the friend countered, "There's no hurry. There's hope for me yet. Remember the thief on the cross?" To which his friend replied, "Yes, but which thief do you want me to remember?"

Your eternal destiny depends on your personal response to Jesus Christ. Will you say, "If you are the Christ . . . "? Or, "Jesus, remember me"?

Positive in Results

The promise that gives paradise is positive in its results. The penitent thief received Jesus' assurance. His plea was answered! "Truly, I say to you, today you will be with me in Paradise."

How loving Jesus' reply! How like him in nature. Faith awakened, cried out. Grace, eternally ready, answered. God's love is always like that. The same love that put Jesus on the cross assures a positive response to all who cry out in faith, believing. Dismas might even have been surprised to receive so positive a result so soon. He only asked to be remembered some day, some distant time when Jesus' kingdom had come. But there was to be no delay. "Today," said Jesus. Shocked or not, Dismas went to his death that day with the positive result of God's love. Those same results would carry him through eternity.

I once heard of a man who prayed, "Oh Lord, give me patience. Now!"

We may pray, "Oh Lord, give me salvation," Jesus answers, "OK, you can have it, full and free and now." That is the positive result of Jesus' death on the cross. He bought our salvation and wants us to have it. Now! Claim that promise for yourself. It's yours in Jesus Christ!

Jesus' second saying from the cross was a promise that gives paradise. One criminal reaped the promise, the other reaped only punishment. It's a perpetual reminder that it's really up to each person to decide what to believe about Jesus. You can repent or not. You can believe or not. You can receive Jesus or not. And on that choice hinges your eternal destiny.

I grew up singing the old gospel song that goes

> Jesus is standing at your heart's door,
> Standing and knocking, He's knocked before;
> This is the question you face once more;
> What will you do with Jesus?
> What will you do with Jesus?
> Neutral you cannot be;
> Some day your heart will be asking,
> "What will He do with me?"[1]

You can claim the promise of paradise for yourself today by trusting Jesus Christ as your personal Savior!

Note

1. B. B. McKinney. Copyright 1940, by The Sunday School Board of the Southern Baptist Convention. Used by permission.

7
The Provision That Radiated Love
John 19:25-27

When Jesus uttered his first words from the cross, he must have looked up as he prayed, "Father, forgive them, for they know not what they do" (Luke 23:34). It was a prayer that gave perspective.

In his second utterance Jesus looked to his side and said to the penitent revolutionary, "Truly, I say unto you, today you will be with me in Paradise" (Luke 23:43). It was a promise that granted access to God.

When he spoke from the cross a third time, Jesus looked down, focusing his feverish eyes on the familiar faces of his mother and beloved disciple. The third word was spoken to them. It was a provision that radiated love. It's recorded only in John 19:25-27. Hear Jesus' third word from the cross.

> But standing by the cross of Jesus were his mother, and his mother's sister, Mary the wife of Clopas, and Mary Magdalene. When Jesus saw his mother, and the disciple whom he loved standing near, he said to his mother, "Woman, behold, your son!" Then he said to the disciple, "Behold, your mother!" And from that hour the disciple took her to his own home.

Love is really what all seven sayings from the cross are all about. In this third word, Jesus radiated love by providing care for his aging mother. Let's look at this third word from the cross, "The Provision That Radiates Love."

Poignant in Pathos

The provision that radiated love is poignant in its pathos. It conveys a depth of feeling we can't even imagine. There's really no way for us to identify with Jesus' suffering on the cross. We can't imagine the extent of it. Yet, in the midst of this dying agony, his thoughts were on his mother's care after he was gone!

And what must Mary's thoughts have been as she watched her son die? Perhaps they flashed momentarily back to Bethlehem, to a stable, shepherds, and a star. Maybe in her reverie she recalled the voices of angels singing to welcome his birth. Or possibly she thought of the words of wise old Simeon at Jesus' dedication in the Temple, when he prophesied that a sword would pierce her soul also. She surely thought her soul was being excised from her body as she watched Jesus in agony. She felt the pain of the nails driven into the hands she'd cared for when they were blistered from Joseph's carpentry shop. It was as if those nails were being driven into her own hands. A thousand times she'd brushed the hair from the brow now pierced with thorns. The spear in his side might as well have been thrust into her own for the pain it caused her. Mary was in agony right along with Jesus.

Rudyard Kipling once wrote:

> If I were hanged on the highest hill,
> *Mother o' mine, O mother o' mine!*
> I know whose love would follow me still,
> Mother o' mine, O mother o' mine!
>
> If I were drowned in the deepest sea,
> Mother o' mine, O mother o' mine!
> I know whose tears would come down to me,
> Mother o' mine, O mother o' mine!

Jesus may have been a criminal to Rome, a blasphemer to Jewish leaders, and a laughingstock to the multitudes, but to Mary he was son. The poignancy of this scene is almost too much for the human emotion. The pathos is beyond comprehension. Jesus suffered, bled, and died. Mary would gladly have exchanged places with him.

Personal Application

Notice the personal application of this provision that radiated love. Jesus spoke directly to Mary and John. In his dying agony, he addressed them as he had spoken directly to the penitent thief and interceded for sinful humanity in his first two words from the cross. He died as he lived, without a thought for himself. To the end he was the man for others, caring personally and directly even in his dying agony.

In the movies the camera can zoom in on a scene so the background and other people fade away. As Jesus addressed Mary and John, all else faded into oblivion. He was speaking directly to the two of them. For a fleeting moment it was as if only the three of them were on the hill.

He spoke to Mary: "Woman, behold, your son!" He wasn't referring to himself. Get the subject of his statement. He didn't say, "Woman, behold your Son!" He was directing Mary's attention now to John, "Woman, behold, your son!" You've got to have both commas there.

Jesus was providing for Mary. For, after he directed her to John, he said to John, "Behold, your mother!" It was as if he'd said, "Look, John will be your son now. He'll take care of you. And John, she will be as a mother to you now. Take care of her."

It means a lot to know that Jesus was personal in his caring. It makes each of us ask ourselves, How caring am I for the needs of others? We can never look at the cross without considering ourselves in light of it. Is there someone you need to care for? someone who needs your love and concern? Don't let life pass by without expressing your love and carrying out your concern with care.

A Picture of Divine Love

This provision is a perfect picture of divine love. The message of the Bible is, "God is love." Every act, word, deed of Jesus' life was motivated by love. The motivating factor behind every word from the cross was love. Divine love is especially demonstrated in this third word. Even in the midst of suffering and death, Jesus' eyes were not dimmed to those he loved most. He expressed his love concretely in caring for Mary. As her eldest son, he fulfilled his responsibility to the uttermost. Why? Love!

I love my mother. I love my wife. I love my children. I love good food. I love animals and the outdoors and sports. I love a good book by a glowing hearth. I love America. Love abounds in life. We use the same word to express our feelings for people, places, things. But there is a love that supersedes all we feel for anyone or anything. It's God's love for us.

When you consider the cross, if you see anything except God's unique love, you've missed the point. The cross is God's final, ultimate demonstration of this love for all in need. That includes you and me.

Though Jesus died on the cross nearly 2,000 years ago, the love that motivated him can still be experienced. As he cared for his mother with dying breath, so he cares for you. Experience his love. Know he cares. Respond to him in faith. Receive him as Savior. Renew yourself in his love by rededicating your life to him. Acknowledge him as Lord. Express your love for him by following him into active discipleship through a local church. His love, like that for his mother, will never let you down!

8
The Feeling of Forsakenness
Mark 15:33-34

To get all seven of Jesus' words from the cross, we must study all four of the Gospels. Luke reported three—the first, "Father, forgive them; for they know not what they do"; the second, "Truly, I say to you, today you will be with me in Paradise"; and the seventh, "Father, into thy hands I commit my spirit!" (23:34,43,46, RSV). John reported three—the third, "Woman, behold, your son!"; "Behold, your mother!"; the fifth, "I thirst"; and the sixth, "It is finished" (6:26-28).

Matthew and Mark report only one word each, and it's the same one, the fourth word from the cross—"My God, my God, why hast thou forsaken me?" Let's see it in context in Mark 15:33-34: "And when the sixth hour had come, there was darkness, over the whole land until the ninth hour. And at the ninth hour Jesus cried with a loud voice, 'Eloi, Eloi, lá ma sabachthani?' which means, 'My God, my God, why hast thou forsaken me?'"

The loneliest feeling in the world is the feeling of forsakenness. It's the emptiness of feeling alone, abandoned, as if no one cared. Jesus had that feeling after six hours on the cross. From noon until 3:00 PM, he hung in total darkness, all nature reflecting the gloom of Golgotha. He suffered in silence those three hours in the dark. When he finally spoke, his fourth saying reflected the darkness of despair he was experiencing. It was "The Feeling of Forsakenness." First, all but one of his family members had forsaken him, then all but one of his disciples had forsaken him, in that hour of darkness Jesus cried out the words he'd learned long ago. "Eloi, Eloi, lá ma sabachthani?"

They are the words of Psalm 22:1. When Jesus spoke them from the cross, he wasn't so much quoting Scripture as expressing his inner thought and emotion. Pious Jews of Jesus' day quoted Psalm 22 in times of distress and adversity. It was a source of encouragement and strength to them. Jesus' use of it doesn't suggest a loss of faith in the Father but the deepest expression of the physical, emotional, and spiritual agony of the cross.

Jesus' fourth word was a cry of desolation, of utter aloneness before God and humanity, taking upon himself the penalty of our sin. It was, in the ultimate sense, "The Feeling of Forsakenness."

Christ's Identification with Us

This feeling of forsakenness is Christ's identification with us. Though we can't fully understand what Jesus went through, we can be sure he knows our occasional feelings of emptiness. We have all felt them in the dark night of despair or the grief of loss or the separation caused by sin. What we must know is that in his dying agony, Jesus experienced every emotion we'll ever have.

Carlyle Marney says of Jesus' fourth word from the cross

> He is not so much calling on God as he is identifying with us in the classic Psalm of the Messiah . . . He says, "Look at what is happening here! This is what it is to be utterly man . . . derelict, desolate, empty . . . this is what it is to be utterly Redeemer." . . . Here Jesus Christ is identifying himself, not with man, but as Man![1]

I think Marney is right. Christ's cry was his identification as one of us. If he were to save to the uttermost, and he does, then he had to encounter the whole, awful range of human experience. His fourth word from the cross is the final step of identification with the extremity of humanity—the feeling of forsakenness!

The author of the Book of Hebrews, who wrote Christ was made "perfect through suffering," bears out this idea in Hebrews 2:17-18:

> Therefore he had to be made like his brethren in every respect, so that he might become a merciful and faithful high priest . . . to make expiation for the sins of the people. For because he himself has suffered and been tempted, he is able to help those who are tempted.

Since Jesus went through the "valley of the shadow" himself, he can help us through our valleys when they come! And they will come. Problems? We will have them. Despair? We will experience it. Forsakenness? We will feel it. But when we do, we have a Comforter and Guide who has been through the darkness and can lead us to the light! The fourth word from the cross is Christ's total identification with our own feelings of forsakenness.

The Cause

In Jesus' darkest hour, he demonstrated the outcome of humanity's sinfulness—separation from God. Jesus had warned about it in his preaching. Then, on our behalf, he experienced it.

The feeling of forsakenness is caused by sin's separation. As Jesus died on the cross, he who knew no sin took our sins upon himself. Sin separates. It separates the sinner from God. This was the great barrier Christ came to break down; but in the process, he felt the ultimate outcome of sin—separation from the Father. His cry "My God, my God, why hast thou forsaken me?" indicates his feeling of forsakenness.

I've heard and read a lot about the meaning of Jesus'

fourth word from the cross. But I've never heard or read anything about the Father's reaction to Jesus' cry. How did God respond to Jesus' feeling of separation, of forsakenness? Was his response indifference? "I told you you'd have to suffer!" No! I think God responded with tears. His heart was broken, just as it is by all sin's separation. Oh, don't you know God wanted to reach out and help Jesus at that precise moment? But to intervene would have been to fail to reconcile humanity to himself. I think God's response to Jesus' cry was, "Though my heart is moved and broken, this is something you must do for humanity. Nobody else can do it!" This is the mystery of God's reconciling love.

Sin separates. All of us know the separation it causes. The sin of youthful rebellion separates youth from parents. The sin of adultery separates husbands and wives. The sin of crime separates the criminal from society by imprisonment, when caught. But most of all, sin separates the sinner from God. I've always thought of sin not so much as breaking God's law, but as breaking God's heart by the separation it causes.

The good news is Christ bore the ultimate separation sin causes; and by accepting his act for us, we need be separated from God by our sins no longer. Jesus saves! The feeling of forsakenness is replaced by the fact of forgiveness for all who receive him.

Not the Final Word

The feeling of forsakenness is not the final word from the cross. Jesus spoke seven times. His cry, "My God, my God, why hast thou forsaken me?" is usually thought to be in the middle, the fourth word. How desolate we would be if this had been his final cry. But a few moments later, he cried out in thirst, then shouted out in triumph before he finally committed his spirit into the hands of the Father.

The cry of despair was not his final word, not forsakenness his final feeling.

This means we will never be left in despair. We are not to harbor the feeling of forsakenness. Oh, yes, there will be times when the sky seems as brass and God does not seem to hear our prayers. When we go through the dark valleys, it may seem as if God doesn't care, isn't moved by our infirmity. But it isn't true! God knows! We know, through Jesus on the cross, our feelings of forsakenness are never our final stop. There's always more beyond—more need, more victory, feelings of presence and assurance, and ultimate triumph yet ahead!

"My God, my God, why hast thou forsaken me?" were Jesus' words of identification with us when he took our sins upon himself. But they were not the final word. Christ cried these words once, now no one else need cry them forever!

Note

1. Carlyle Marney, *He Became Like Us* (New York: Abingdon Press, 1964), p. 47.

9
The Cry of Need
John 19:28-29

Every parent knows the experience of a thirsty child at bedtime. They have been tucked in, prayed with, and kissed good-night. For the first time all day you relax, get your feet up, and your shoes off. You grab the evening paper—a moment just for yourself.

That's when it comes.

"I'm thirsty!"

At first you ignore it, hoping maybe you didn't really hear it. But the second time you are addressed personally. "Mommy (or Daddy), I'm thirsty!"

"No you're not. Go to sleep!"

"I can't go to sleep, I'm thirsty."

Then you feel a little tinge of guilt and wonder if the child really is thirsty. So you get up and take the child some water. If you have two children, the second one inevitably gets thirsty at that precise moment. They are then quenched, retucked, and rekissed. Sometimes that's the end of it. They really were thirsty. If they wet the beds, you know they really weren't.

Thirst is a universal, physical need. You can die of dehydration quicker than just about anything else. All of us have been thirsty and can probably remember the thirstiest we've ever been.

But no matter how thirsty we've been, it's not likely we've had a thirst that wasn't easily quenched. We've never had a thirst like Jesus' thirst on the cross that occasioned his fifth word. John 19:28-29 gives the record of Jesus' cry of need: "After this Jesus, knowing that all was now finished, said (to fulfil the scripture), 'I thirst.' A bowl full of vinegar stood there; so they put a sponge full of the vinegar on hyssop and held it to his mouth."

Jesus' first saying on the cross was a prayer that gave perspective. His second was a promise of paradise. Next came provision for his mother. Then, the cry of his soul expressed his spiritual suffering. Now we come to the fifth word, the agony of Christ's body, his physical suffering. Oh, he'd been suffering all along, all right. In fact, the fifth word came only after Jesus met the needs of the world in the first word, the needs of the person dying next to him in the second word, and the needs of his mother in the third word. He thought of himself last! How characteristic of Jesus. How utterly selfless he was.

"I thirst," was Jesus' plaintive cry of need from the cross. It was uttered from his parched throat and lips as the end of life for him approached at about 3:00 PM.

Let's look at this "Cry of Need" and see just what needs are represented in it and what insight it gives us for living.

Physical Need

The fifth word is a cry of physical need. The most direct meaning of the fifth word from the cross is the most obvious—it shows his full humanity. We tend to overidealize Jesus, to vaporize his humanness. But he was fully human. There can be no doubt of that when you hear him cry, "I thirst."

Many commentators spiritualize the meaning of the fifth word. They say it is Christ's identification with humanity or that it shows all our needs are known to him or that he meant he thirsted after righteousness or that he was just fulfilling Scripture in this word. But I believe Jesus cried, "I thirst," because he was literally physically thirsty. Besides, Jesus would never have faked thirst for any reason. He thirsted and cried out in his need.

For his first three hours on the cross he hung in the scorching morning sun. Then for nearly three hours he suffered in silence. Once the anguish of his soul expressed his feeling of forsakenness, the full realization of his physical suffering burst upon him; he cried out in need, "I thirst!"

This Jesus—sinless perfection, only begotten Son of God, second person of the Holy Trinity—was fully man and in his dying agony was consumed with burning thirst.

People will steal for food, but they'll kill for water. We can live a long time without food (especially those of us who have an abundance of body fat stored up). Mahatma Gandhi is a reminder that we can live quite a while without eating. But we soon die if there's nothing to drink.

Jesus was thirsty. His cry of need does show his humanity, his physical need. But we must also remember, this cry came from a cross. He was dying there for the sins of the world. This includes you and me. His intense physical thirst was caused by relieving others of spiritual thirst. And because Jesus went to that cross for us, no one ever need thirst spiritually again. Remember that when you consider the cross and the Christ upon it.

What are you thirsty for today? Life? You can find it in abundance in Jesus who died for you. Forgiveness? He paid for your sins on the cross. Righteousness? All things were made right by him. Whatever your need, it can be satisfied by Jesus. That's the message of the cross—the man who died there can meet your needs.

Prophetic Fulfillment

This cry met the need of prophetic fulfillment. John wrote, "After this, Jesus, knowing that all was now finished, said (to fulfil the scripture), 'I thirst.'" John's parenthetical comment is important. He said, "to fulfil the scripture." That wasn't so much the purpose of the fifth word from the cross as the result. For, when Jesus cried, "I thirst," he was fulfilling the prophecy of Psalm 22:15. He'd already quoted Psalm 22:1, "Then he fulfilled a prophecy from this messianic psalm, My strength has dried up like sun-baked clay, my tongue sticks to my mouth, for you have laid me in the dust of death" (TLB). He was also fulfilling the prophecy of Psalm 69:21, "They gave me also gall for my meat; and in my thirst they gave me vinegar to drink."

Every prophecy of the Messiah in the Old Testament was fulfilled by Jesus. Thus, the crying need of the world for the Redeemer, the Holy One of God, the promised Messiah is fully met in Jesus Christ.

From the time humanity sinned in the Garden of Eden, God had promised reconciliation. In Jesus, it was made possible. He is the fulfillment of all God's promises and all mankind's needs.

Think of all the needs of humanity that have ever existed. The thought staggers the mind! List them. The list is inexhaustible. There are psychological needs—the need for acceptance, recognition, love, and security. There are spiritual needs—forgiveness, faith, grace, and joy, independent of circumstances. There are relational needs—the longing for fellowship, patience, gentleness, kindness, meekness, and goodness. There are personal needs—self-understanding, self-acceptance, self-control, and peace of mind.

How are our needs met? Ultimately, only one way. Our needs are met through Jesus Christ. All other routes are dead-end streets. He is the way, both the means and end to having all our needs met. God said it would be so and it is!

Put your faith and trust in Jesus Christ, God's Promised One. He's able to meet all your needs as faithfully as he fulfilled God's promises and the Scripture's prophecies.

Personal Dependence

As Jesus hung in dying agony, he had to cry out to others to assuage his thirst. He was still the embodiment of power. He still was charged with full authority over heaven and earth. Yet, as he died, he cried out to those responsible for putting him on the cross to quench his thirst. Even Jesus needed help in his darkest hour.

Someone there helped him. Perhaps it was a Roman soldier or a Jewish boy there to watch the spectacle—somebody offered him a sponge soaked with some wine to cool his burning lips and soak his parched throat. I believe this drink was offered in compassion, not in cruelty. It was a tiny island of compassion in a sea of suffering.

Let me ask you a question. Of all the people standing at the cross, were you there who would you rather have been? A Roman legionnaire gambling for Jesus' clothing? A Jewish bigwig jeering in jest? His brokenhearted mother watching her son suffer to death? A disillusioned disciple with dashed dreams?

No, I think the person any one of us would rather have been was whoever gave the suffering Savior the quenching drink!

This act of kindness should say to all of us that none of us live to ourselves and none die to ourselves. We are inexorably linked one to another and dependent on each other.

We all have needs, physical and spiritual, we cannot meet by ourselves. For our spiritual needs, we're totally dependent on God. For our physical needs we're, at least partially, dependent on others.

Today let God meet your spiritual needs through Jesus Christ. Give yourself trustingly to him, and he will build within you the confidence you need in others. We all need it. Even Jesus on the cross shows us that.

The cry of need was, "I thirst." It shows us physical need, prophetic fulfillment, and personal dependence. It also tells us God can meet all our needs if we will trust him. Let him come into you today to save you, renew you, challenge you, bless you. He can meet all your cries of need!

10
The Shout of Triumph
John 19:30

Had we been at the foot of Jesus' cross we surely would have noticed that his seven words took very different forms. The fifth word, "I thirst," was a cry, replete with physical suffering, a body aching with agony and aflame with thirst.

The fourth word was an expression of anguish, addressed to God. Had we been in the curious crowd we could barely have heard him at all when he sighed, "My God, why?"

The third word was very personal, spoken to his beloved mother and devoted disciple. We would have felt like we were eavesdropping if we'd overheard it.

The second word was a promise directed to an individual in response to repentance and faith.

The first word was a prayer—Christ making intercession for the forgiveness of sins.

Now we come to the sixth word. It's the most unique among the seven. John 19:30 says, "When Jesus had received the vinegar, he said, 'It is finished'; and he bowed his head and gave up his spirit."

"It is finished." That's what Jesus said. But how he said it constitutes its uniqueness. Was it the moan of defeat in death, "It's all over"? Was it a sigh of relief and resignation, "I've done it, finally"?

No! It was a shout! A shout of triumph. Jesus died with the voice of victory emanating from his pain-racked body.

He was not overcome by death but was an overcomer of death. No one took his life from him. He laid it down willingly, voluntarily, victoriously. No wonder "It is finished" is the supreme shout of triumph of our Savior.

Let's look at this sixth word from the cross, this shout of triumph, a single word in the Greek language, and see what it signifies to us.

Christ's Work Done

The shout of triumph signified that Jesus' work was done. We've probably all heard that when persons near death, their whole lives flash before them in a twinkle. Perhaps, between the drink of vinegar and the shout of triumph, Jesus' mind flashed back to all Mary had "kept in her heart" and told him of Bethlehem and his birth. Maybe his mind's eye beheld Joseph's carpentry shop in Nazareth or his own baptism in the Jordan River or the terrible temptations in the wilderness. Perhaps he remembered, if only for an instant, the miracles, the people, the teachings of his all too brief ministry. All this had led to where he was, dying on a cross. But he realized he hung not in defeat but triumph.

He shouted, "It is finished." His public ministry and saving work was completed. This was a victor's shout by one who ran the full race, won the struggle, came out of the darkness into the light, and grasped the crown.

Jesus had done what only he could do. The completely unique work of redemption was accomplished, and he veritably shouted in triumph.

Picture if you can a man who can't swim falling into a deep lake. Then try to picture representatives of various religions coming by, and how they might respond to the drowning man.

Confucius might say to him, "Profit by your experience."

Buddha might console him by saying, "Life is suffering

and suffering leads to enlightenment."

Hinduism would say, "You may have better opportunity in your next incarnation."

Muhammed might tell the drowning man, "Whether you live or survive, it is the will of Allah!"

How would Jesus respond? I believe he would say, "Here, take my hand, I'll pull you out!"

On the cross Jesus did for us what no one else could. He provided the way out of sin and into salvation. "It is finished" means he did all he came to do. For this cause he came into the world.

Have you reached out and taken his hand? He's holding it out to you. But you must take it by faith. Grab hold of him today as your Savior. That's why he came to earth. That's why he died. That's what the cross means. That's what Jesus did for you!

Salvation's Won

The sixth word from the cross is a single word as Jesus shouted it. Transliterated in Greek it's *tetelestai*. It's a perfect passive indicative verb meaning, "it has been completed and remains finished." In the New Testament, it was used three ways. It means to bring to an end, finish, or complete. It means to carry out, accomplish, fulfill, or perform. In business it means to pay or "paid in full." All of these meanings apply to Jesus' shout of this word from the cross.

When Jesus shouted *tetelestai,* he was signifying to God, "Your purpose in sending me to reconcile humanity to yourself is accomplished, fulfilled, completed." But he was also signifying to all people for all time, "The price for your sin is fully paid. The way for you to God is opened up through me. Your sins are atoned for. Access to God is possible. It's finished, accomplished, performed."

A father and son were members of a hunting party in

the frozen wasteland of Antarctica. Trekking across an ice floe, the son was suddenly separated from his father as the ice cracked between them. The boy screamed in terror as the piece of ice on which he stood began to float away. Panic-stricken, the father stood in frozen inaction.

Another member of the party responded quickly to the dire situation. He ran over to the edge of the main body of ice and, fully extending himself, lunged for the breakaway piece of ice. Barely spanning the breach he grasped onto it by his fingertips, the chilling waters lapping over his body.

"Walk over me," he shouted. "Walk over me like a bridge, to safety." And the trembling boy soon found himself safely in the arms of his father.

In his saving act of dying on the cross, Jesus formed the bridge to God on our behalf. No wonder he could shout in triumph! Jesus sent a message to the world on that first Good Friday that said, "Nothing more is needed for your salvation from my end. It is finished. Walk over me like a bridge, to salvation. The Father awaits you with open arms."

Our Work's Begun

The shout of triumph signifies that our work has just begun. "It is finished" means God has done all he could to make himself known to mankind. It also means Jesus has done all he could to open the way to God and identify with us. His work is done, salvation's won from the divine side. Now it's up to us. The salvation process is completed by our faith.

And not only that but also it's up to us to tell others what Jesus did for them until every person on earth has heard the good news of Jesus Christ. That's our bold mission and must be the thrust of our lives. The cross of Christ is the highest expression of God's love. We must share that love and take up our cross and follow him.

The happiest feeling in the world is experiencing faith in Jesus Christ for the first time. The only thing I know that even roughly equates is leading someone else to know him. Oh, the joy of doing the work God gave us to do!

Do you want to know what Jesus, God's Son, was doing on a cross, shouting, "It is finished"? He was redeeming humanity. But until everybody knows that, we still have work to do! Give yourself to God. Go with him and go for him, all the way. That's how far he went for you. When he shouted *tetelestai,* it meant his work was done; salvation's won; our work's begun. You too can shout in triumph when you truly experience the victorious Christ!

11
The Word That Shows the Way
Luke 23:44-46

Had we been at the cross we'd have heard Jesus' final word:

> It was now about the sixth hour, and there was darkness over the whole land until the ninth hour, while the sun's light failed; and the curtain of the temple was torn in two. Then Jesus, crying with a loud voice, said, "Father, into thy hands I commit my spirit!" And having said this he breathed his last (Luke 23:44-46).

The agony of the cross was over. Jesus died in record time, only six hours. Sometimes it took days to die by crucifixion. To Jesus and his mother, it may have seemed an eternity. In those six agonizing hours, Jesus spoke seven times. Each word revealed more and more of his mind and thoughts. Each word showed God more clearly. Each word brought salvation nearer humanity.

Jesus went through words of intercession, promise, provision, forsakenness, physical suffering, and triumph to the final word of commitment. He died as he lived, totally committed to the Father.

Jesus' first and last words had some striking similarities and some vast differences. As the first word was a prayer to the Father, so was the seventh. They began with the same word of endearment, "Father." But the first word was spoken softly. The seventh was shouted. The first was intercessory. The last was dedicatory. The first word shows love. The final word shows the way love leads.

Look at the seventh word from the cross. I call it "The Word That Shows the Way." Look at the way it shows for us to walk.

The Way to the Father

Jesus came to earth to reveal God the Father to humanity. He came to restore and reconcile us to the Father. With his final breath, he showed the way to the Father, through commitment. "Father, into *thy* hands I commit my spirit!" (author's italics).

This was Jesus' final commitment. All his life commitment characterized Jesus' relationship to God. Every word, deed, prayer, and interpersonal encounter testified to Jesus' commitment to God. In his final moment of life, he opened the way to God by his commitment.

That Jesus shows us the way to God is symbolized in verse 45, "the curtain of the temple was torn in two." This was the veil (curtain) separating the holy place from the holy of holies. The Jews believed that behind this curtain of purple and scarlet linen dwelt the very presence of God himself. Only the high priest of Israel had access into the holy of holies and he only one day per year (Yom Kippur, the "Day of Atonement"). The curtain was tremendous in size. But the symbolic separation between God and common people was even thicker.

But when Jesus died, he opened the way to God. The curtain, the barrier of separation, was torn from top to bottom. The way to God was opened—forever! No longer an inaccessible "God in a box," through Jesus Christ the way to the Father was opened to every repenting and believing sinner for all time. Jesus is the way to communion with the Father now and forever.

The Way to Live

Not only did Jesus show us the way to the Father but the seventh word from the cross also shows the way to live.

Jesus died as he lived—committed to God. "Father, into thy hands I commit [commend, KJV] my spirit." He lived with a daily sense of God's watchcare and provision, and he died in that train of thought.

Several commentators suggest this seventh word may have been Jesus' daily prayer. It was a quotation of Psalm 31:5, with only the word "Father" added. This was the evening prayer for all Jewish children, much as ours pray, "Now I lay me down to sleep, I pray the Lord my soul to keep . . . "

Jesus uttered it as his last thought before he died. Jesus lived with God's Word daily. He knew the Old Testament. It gave him strength and insight for daily living. He often quoted it. He drew upon it as a resource in teaching. In the last breath of life, he found peace, security, and fulfillment in saying his boyhood prayer one final time.

Thinking on this I wrote,

When the furor of life was over,
And his work on earth was done,
Our Savior recalled the boyhood prayer,
His lips had often sung.
"Into thy hands," he trustingly prayed,
"I commend my spirit."
Then breathing his last, he died that day,
The Father's house to inherit.

Oh, if we would only live with the same sense of commitment, with God's Word daily, we could live more like Jesus. Committing ourselves in love and obedience to him results in peace, contentment, and security. Trust God. Deliver yourself over to him completely, as Jesus did. He shows us the way to live.

The Way To Die

Jesus died trusting God. Jesus committed his spirit to God, a reminder that his death wasn't a catastrophe or fatality or an accident, but the climax and consummation of a divine plan. For this hour he had come. Therefore he yielded himself to God in confident trust. Thus, he died as he lived and shows us the way to do both.

People generally die as they live. You know the old saying, "If you live by the sword, you'll die by the sword." Recently I watched a friend die. She died as she lived—in peace, beauty, and serenity.

In everything Jesus said and did, he taught us how to live. With his final word, he taught us how to die. Most people die as they live. So live as you wish to die.

If you live with God's Word as your constant companion and guide, God's will as your daily commitment, God's way as your daily path, then there will be comfort and security as your pillow when you lay down your head in death. Decide now that Jesus is the way. He's the way to live. He's the way to die. Follow him and you'll never go wrong!

Now that you see the way, don't you want to take it? Jesus is the way to the Father, the way to live, the way to die. What a way to go! Go with him. Follow him.

Think back with me over "Those Seven Words."

"Father, forgive them . . . "
Hear him plead it,
In words so quiet and low,
From Calvary's tree,
For you and me,
Did ever love speak so?

"Today you'll be with me . . . "
Hear him say it,
In words assured, yet pained.
One thief spurned,
The other turned,
And paradise he gained.

"Behold, your son . . . "

Hear him provide,
In words of comfort and love,
To Mary dear,
To John her care,
'Til they should meet above.

"My God, my God . . . "
Hear his anguish,
In words of desolation.
But God was there,
In love did care,
To bring him consolation.

"I thirst . . . "
Hear him cry it,
In words of suffering sore.
They gave him wine,
Those sins of mine,
Helped cause the pain he bore.

"It is finished . . . "
Hear him shout it,
In words so clear and bold.
His work is done,
Salvation's won,
The whole world must be told!

"Father, into thy hands . . . "
Hear him pray it,
In words of commendation.
He'd reached the end,
'Til he rose again,
To bring the world salvation!

Section II

Were You There . . . At the Resurrection?

12
The Greatest Word in the World
Mark 16:1-7

Had you been at the foot of the cross you would have heard Jesus speak some of the greatest words in human history. He spoke seven times. In his words, we hear a prayer for forgiveness, the assurance of heaven, a picture of love—human and divine, the full range of spiritual and physical feelings he experienced, the humaneness of Jesus, the completion of his life and work, and the way to live and die.

One of the greatest words in the world wasn't spoken by Jesus, but about him. And it wasn't at the cross. It was at the open tomb. Had you been at the scene of the empty tomb you might have heard this word. An angel announced it to the women who'd come to anoint Jesus' body. That word which rings out the greatest good news ever told is one word in the Greek language—*ēgerthē*. It's translated by three words into English—"He has risen!"

This word is recorded in the resurrection narratives in both Matthew and Mark. Mark was probably the first written account:

> And when the sabbath was past, Mary Magdalene, Mary the mother of James, and Salome bought spices, so that they might go and anoint him. And very early on the first day of the week they went to the tomb when the sun had risen. And they were saying to one another, "Who will roll away the stone for us from the door of the tomb?" And looking up, they saw that the stone was rolled back—it was

> very large. And entering the tomb, they saw a young man sitting on the right side, dressed in a white robe; and they were amazed. And he said to them, "Do not be amazed; you seek Jesus of Nazareth, who was crucified. He has risen, he is not here; see the place where they laid him. But go, tell his disciples and Peter that he is going before you to Galilee; there you will see him, as he told you" (16:1-7).

"He has risen!" *Ēgerthē.* Wrapped up in this one word is a whole world of theology and meaning. To study just this word involves the whole realm of the language of our New Testament and confirms the truth that this is indeed the greatest word in the world.

Centers on a Person

The greatest word in the world centers on a person. "*He* has risen!" Jesus is the subject of the greatest word in the world. The resurrection begins and ends with Jesus Christ. It took him to fill this word with meaning and importance.

Jesus did many great things in life. He worked miracles. He touched untouchables. He changed lives. He even raised the dead.

Jesus said many great things. He painted word pictures, describing his followers as salt and light. He set forth great principles, like "Do unto others." He graphically described his kingdom in the Beatitudes. He delineated the greatest commandment, "Thou shalt love the Lord thy God . . . "

Jesus showed many great things during his life, love, compassion, forgiveness, truth. He embodied them all.

But he died. Just like all other great men—religious leaders, prophets, and priests—he died. So if his story ended there, he'd be just another great man who did, said, and showed great things.

But Jesus wasn't just great. He was the greatest! And this is clearly seen in the subject of the greatest word in the world—"*He* has risen!" Jesus rose from death back to life.

The announcement of that good news then became the greatest word in the world because it can be said of no one else. Jesus is the sum and substance of the good news.

Have you ever stopped to think how dangerous it is to put all your confidence in individuals other than Jesus? No matter how dear, true, or fine they may be—be they teacher, parents, pastors, doctors, children, or friends—they can let you down. Beware of centering your life on a person. That person will let you down.

But not Jesus! He's the one person you can center everything on with perfect trust, confidence, and reliability. He conquered death. Therefore, he conquered life. He wants to give you life and the only way you can have it is to make him the center of your life. The good news centers on a person—Jesus Christ.

Describes an Action

The greatest word in the world describes an action. *Ēgerthē* is a verb. It's a simple aorist or past-tense verb. It describes something that has been done. But it's a passive voice verb, that is, it describes the action of the subject being acted on. The subject is Jesus. The action—"He *has* risen!" This denotes the eternal fact of the resurrection. Jesus was raised from death to life by the power of God. This action established Jesus as unique forever. The resurrection of Jesus Christ from the grave is an eternal fact, that's what this verb means. From that moment to this it can be said of Jesus, "He *has* risen!"

George W. Cornell is a reporter for the Associated Press. In a widely-circulated newspaper article, he analyzed the journalistic integrity of the resurrection narratives. He looked at the various accounts from the standpoint of their diversity, central consistency, uncoordinated accounts, accounts in the remainder of the New Testament, and their impact on the style and content of the New Testament. He concluded, "What is reported offers journalistic evidence of the authenticity of the accounts. They weren't doctored to be precise. . . . They convey the startling conclusion that Jesus, though killed, lives!"[1]

The resurrection of Jesus is an eternal fact. But it's not proven by journalistic analysis or scientific investigation. It's proven by the experience of faith in the life of the believer and borne out in faithful living day by day.

The action of the resurrection means that because he has risen we too can know life. We can share that action!

Assures a Result

The greatest word in the world assures a result. "He has *risen*!" The mood of a verb indicates the relation of the action to reality. The indicative mood, the mood of this greatest of words *ēgerthē*, confirms the reality of the action from the viewpoint of the speaker. In other words, when the angel announced Jesus had risen it meant he was alive forevermore. The result of the action of resurrection was assured by the force of the verb.

Easter brings the assurance of life. Death couldn't contain Jesus. "He has *risen*!" The result is assured. Death was defeated by life.

During the Revolutionary War, George Washington and his ragtag army crossed a bridge over the Brandywine River in northern Delaware. An aide asked him, "General, what shall we do with the bridge?" Washington thought for a moment. Then he told the aide, "Burn it! Let us make no provision for retreat. It is now victory or death!"

With the resurrection of Jesus Christ from the dead, no provision was made for retreat. The result of life, abundant now and eternal, was assured. That's the meaning and message of Easter.

Jesus is the resurrection and the life. He who believes in Jesus, though he may die, yet shall he live. And whosoever lives and believes in Jesus will never die! (See John 11:25-26.) This is the assurance of faith in Jesus Christ and the result he assures to all who believe.

Because Jesus rose, you do not have to be defeated by sin and death. Through faith centered in him, you can accept the eternal fact of his resurrection and receive the assurance of life.

That's the message of Easter. That's the meaning of this greatest word in the world—"He has risen!" Give your life to him, your faith, your all, and you can live with the living Lord!

Note

1. George W. Cornell, *Houston Chronicle*, 10 April 1977.

13
The Greatest Event in Human History
Matthew 28:1-7

"Were you there when He rose up from the dead?" This is the poignant question asked in an old Negro Spiritual. Had we been at the resurrection we would have witnessed the greatest event in human history!

Have you ever stopped to consider what was the greatest thing that ever happened? Surely out of the great events in the history of humanity, one must be the greatest.

Some might suggest one of the great empires constituted the most significant event. Egypt, Assyria, Babylon, Persia, Greece, Rome, the modern European Common Market, and the United States of America would all be contenders for greatness. Yet, to me, the greatest event was not an empire.

Others would think the world's greatest event was a person like Abraham, Aristotle, Plato, Helen of Troy, Philip or Alexander the Great, Paul, Napoleon, Washington, Jefferson, Lincoln or Churchill. Great as these are, I still don't think it's a person.

Many might name some adventurer or inventor or discoverer as the greatest. Oh, the world has seen exciting pathfinders from before Columbus to modern astronauts. And who could deny the greatness of Edison, George Washington Carver, Madam Curie, or William Jenner? Yet, I submit the greatest event was not one of their discoveries.

Of all events in history, the single greatest is the resurrection of Jesus Christ from the grave! From the standpoint of things that really count, things of eternal significance, all other events shrink in importance beside the resurrection. It's more important than any other single event because it did what none other could do—it brought ultimate life, salvation, and hope to all people everywhere for all time and eternity! The unmistakable greatness of the resurrection cannot be denied!

It's the event we celebrate at Easter. And not on that day only, the first day of every week Christians celebrate the resurrection of Christ. The Bible tells about this greatest of all events in the simplest of reportage. Here's the account from Matthew 28:1-7:

> Now after the sabbath, toward the dawn of the first day of the week, Mary Magdalene and the other Mary went to see the sepulchre. And behold, there was a great earthquake; for an angel of the Lord descended from heaven and came and rolled back the stone, and sat upon it. His appearance was like lightning, and his raiment white as snow. And for fear of him the guards trembled and became like dead men. But the angel said to the women, "Do not be afraid; for I know that you seek Jesus who was crucified. He is not here; for he has risen, as he said. Come, see the place where he lay. Then go quickly and tell his disciples that he has risen from the dead, and behold, he is going before you to Galilee; there you will see him. Lo, I have told you."

There are three observations I want to make about the resurrection.

Centers on Jesus

The greatest event in human history centers on the Godman, Jesus Christ. He's what the Easter event is all about. Jesus is the center and circumference of this greatest of all episodes in the annals of time.

Mary Magdalene is not centrally important here, fascinating as she may be. Matthew certainly gave her a leading role in the Easter drama. She is prominently and personally mentioned. But she's not the star!

The angel of annuciation wasn't the central figure here either. His role was important. As God's messenger, he had the privilege of announcing the good news. But he was just the enunciator of the central figure.

It wasn't the joyous disciples, thrilled beyond belief at the word they received.

No, the star of the Easter drama wasn't even at the scene! He was risen! Nevertheless, Jesus was the central figure of the resurrection. And the fact that he was gone from the tomb is the greatest single fact in history! In comparison, persons around the tomb weren't important. The place was comparatively unimportant. The time was fairly insignificant. The person Jesus Christ is what's important about Easter. "He has risen," is the good news. By his death and resurrection, he became the Redeemer of humanity. Christianity centers in the living Christ!

The French statesman Charles Talleyrand was noted for his craftiness. It is said that one day he engaged in conversation a fellow countryman who wanted to start a new religion. It was to be a grand faith, amalgamating the best of all the world's great religions and eliminating what he considered to be their weaknesses. But he was having a tough time. No converts had been made. He'd worked hard. He just couldn't find many interested. He asked Talleyrand what he should do.

Talleyrand replied that he hardly knew what to advise. He acknowledged the extreme difficulty of such a task.

"Still," Talleyrand said after a brief pause, "there's at least one plan you should try. Why don't you get yourself crucified and rise again on the third day?"

The length, breadth, height, and depth of our message and faith is that Jesus, who died on a cross and was sealed in a tomb, is alive. This is the central fact and he is the central figure in this greatest event.

Focuses on Life

The greatest event in human history focuses on life. Why do people attend church on Easter in greater numbers than on any other day of the year? Some would say because it's a tradition to go to church on Easter. Others would say they come out of a sense of guilt for not attending regularly through the year. Their consciences won't permit them to lay out on Easter!

But I think more people are in church on Easter than any other day because Easter focuses on life. The consummate meaning of Jesus' resurrection is life. Life here and now, life hereafter.

Can you imagine the power of God operative in Jesus to bring him back to life after he died? That's power! That's life! And that's the focus of this event. It's what makes it the greatest in history.

Someone once told me, "If you're born once you die twice. But if you're born twice you die once." What that means is, if you're only born physically, you die both physically and spiritually. But if you're born physically then reborn spiritually, you die only physically. Spiritually you live forever.

This is borne out in the resurrection event. It's proof positive that life is possible beyond death. If God could give Jesus life after death, he will do it for you and me, as he said. The focus of Easter is on life.

Calls for Response

The greatest event in human history calls for a personal response from each of us. In the message of Matthew's glad narrative, there are three imperative verbs which call for action, response. They are, "Do not be afraid," "Come, see," and "go quickly and tell."

"Do not be afraid" is an affirmation of God's control of life, death, and faith. It calls for the response of trust in God's provision. We don't understand the mysteries of life and death, but God does. Trust him, then there's no need to fear.

"Come, see" is an invitation to examine the reality, the proof of the resurrection. Some deny its reality. But the response of faith is to receive the truth of the empty tomb on the testimony of those who went and saw. The tomb was empty. And over five hundred people were eyewitnesses to the living Christ after the resurrection. Proof enough. Open your spiritual eyes in response and you too can know the reality of this greatest event in history.

"Go quickly and tell," calls for the response of sharing, of fulfilling the Great Commission. It's our job to bear the good news of this great event to a dying world. It's light. It's life. It's hope. And all of these the world needs. Who'll go and tell if you don't?

How like life and Christianity is this call for response to the living Lord. It begins with faith, belief. It proceeds to firm knowledge, Christian growth, commitment. It culminates in sharing, witnessing to this mighty act of God.

What would you have done had you been at the empty tomb that day? We don't really know, do we? But I suspect we would have had the impulse to run through the streets shouting, "He is alive! He has risen! He's alive!"

If you see the same empty tomb today with your inner eyes, the same response is appropriate. The resurrection of Jesus Christ, the greatest event in human history demands a response. Trusting, knowing, and sharing are the three basic elements of our Christian faith.

This Lord of life calls for our lives. Today can become the greatest day in your life if the greatest event in human history becomes real to you!

14
The Day Death Died
Luke 23:55 to 24:8

Had we been disciples of Jesus during his earthly ministry, the cross would have loomed large in our minds. In fact, it still does. The cross is the central symbol of Christianity. We display it in our churches. We wear it in forms of gold and silver. The cross is about death, a reminder Jesus died for us.

There was no need to remind Jesus' disciples of that. They watched him die. Death was on their minds. Dead was the person who claimed kinship to God. Dead were the hopes, dreams, and enthusiasm of his followers. Dead was the promise of a new life of love and salvation. All these things died with Jesus. Death was in the air.

But those who loved Jesus in life were determined to care for his dead body. It was about 3:00 PM on Friday when Jesus died. The sabbath officially began at sundown, about 6:00 PM. So Joseph of Arimathea had to hurry to get Jesus' body down from the cross and buried before the sabbath, after Pilate gave him permission.

> The women who had come with Jesus from Galilee followed Joseph and saw the tomb and how his body was laid in it. Then they went home and prepared spices and perfumes. But they rested on the Sabbath in obedience to the commandment.
>
> On the first day of the week, very early in the morning, the women took the spices they had prepared and went to the tomb. They found the stone rolled away from the tomb,

> but when they entered, they did not find the body of the Lord Jesus. While they were wondering about this, suddenly two men in clothes that gleamed like lightning stood beside them. In their fright the women bowed down with their faces to the ground, but the men said to them, "Why do you look for the living among the dead? He is not here; he has risen! Remember how he told you, while he was still with you in Galilee: 'The Son of Man must be delivered into the hands of sinful men, be crucified and on the third day be raised again.'" Then they remembered his words (Luke 23:55 to 24:8, NIV).

This is Luke's account of the first Easter, resurrection day. I call it "the day death died." The reason I call it this is because of the angel's question to the women at the tomb, "Why do you look for the living among the dead?" (Luke 24:5). Luke alone reports this question. I believe it gives a unique perspective to the meaning of the resurrection.

Death claimed Jesus on the cross. But he conquered death at the resurrection. Easter, then, becomes "the day death died."

Christ Himself Came Alive

Easter is the day death died because Christ himself came alive. The angel asked, "Why do you look for the living among the dead?" Then he announced, "He is not here; he has risen!" The word translated "the living," is literally "the living One." It's a unique reference to the risen Christ. The emphatic pronouns, "*He* is not here; *he* has risen," give added impetus to Jesus Christ as the central figure of the resurrection.

The resurrection isn't about an event, significant as the event is. It isn't about a holiday, wonderful as that holiday has become. The resurrection is about a person, Jesus Christ, who died and was buried and rose from death to new life. His life, death, and resurrection are the final and ultimate proof of God's love and victory over sin and death.

Early Christians made much of the fact that Jesus' body wasn't in the tomb—that he actually, literally rose from the grave. The reason they did so was that certain theories erupted that Jesus didn't actually come back to life. Some charged that his disciples had stolen his body. Others theorized that the women went to the wrong tomb. Some maintained that Jesus didn't really die on the cross in the first place, he only swooned or fainted. They say he was actually alive when sealed in the cave. Still others persist that the whole resurrection episode was some kind of a hallucination, a figment of someone's imagination.

But the testimony of Scripture bears out the angel's announcement, "the living One is not here among the dead—Jesus is alive again" (author's paraphrase).

There was no body! Jesus himself came alive. This is the first fact in any consideration of him as Lord. It's also the major factor separating Christianity from all other major world religions. It's also the major tenet of belief for salvation. Romans 10:9 says, "If you confess with your lips that Jesus is Lord and believe in your heart that God raised him from the dead, you will be saved."

Christ himself came alive and dealt the final blow to death forever. Jesus is the Living One! No bonds of death or grave could keep him. This is the good news of Easter.

Christ's Words Came Alive

Death died on Easter when Christ's words came alive. Those who went to the tomb on Sunday morning weren't seeking a risen Lord. They went to anoint a dead body. The angel's question, "Why do you seek the living among the dead?" (RSV), was a mild rebuke to the women for not remembering Jesus' predictions of his resurrection. Though he had spoken often of it, they couldn't grasp the idea. They didn't expect it. Therefore they were surprised to find no body in the tomb.

They shouldn't have been. No less than a dozen times

he'd told his followers he would rise again. "Destroy this temple and I will raise it again in three days", he had said (John 2:19, NIV). He'd spoken of it in Luke 9; 18, and in Matthew, Mark, and John.

Yet, it took the words of the angel, "Remember how he told you," to awaken their spiritual sensitivities to the truth of Jesus' words. But, oh, how those words came alive that day!

There's no way we can measure the miracle of the resurrection. To what could we compare it? Nothing in human experience equals it. It's beyond human comprehension.

Think of our own experience with death. We can't conceive of a loved one dying, being buried, and then going out to visit the grave, finding it open, the body gone, and discovering the person alive again. It's beyond imagination. But that's what happened with Jesus.

And when you add the element that he said it would happen and it happened exactly as he foretold, then I say with utter certainty death died when Christ's words came alive!

However, we can't be too hard on the women at the tomb. Surely they believed him, but perhaps just didn't expect it so soon. Maybe they thought of a glorious resurrection at the end of time. Who would ever have thought of an empty tomb on that Sunday morning?

Only Jesus! He said three days and meant it. That's what makes it so special. He came alive, his words came alive, and death died.

Christ's Promises Came Alive

The day death died Jesus' promises came alive. Verse 8 is redemptive in implication. "Then they remembered his words." Jesus had not only predicted his resurrection but he also promised life to his followers. Surely then as they remembered his prophecies, his promises also took on new meaning for them. "Then they remembered his words."

When they found the tomb empty and when the angels announced the great good news of his resurrection and reminded them of Jesus' words, surely a light brightened their despondency and again they could hear all the words of the Savior.

"Hope" took on new meaning at the resurrection,
"Faith" took on added depth,
"Love" reached a new dimension,
"Peace" took an extra step.

Death died at Easter and Christ's promises came alive to all who believe.

A little boy wrote a letter to God.

DEAR GOD,

What is it like when you die? Nobody will tell me. I just want to know. I don't want to do it.

Your friend,
MIKE

All of us would like to know what it's like to die, but we don't want to die to find out. There's been a lot of research lately into death and dying. Many stories have surfaced about people who were clinically dead but revived. Our curiosity is awakened by death. What is it like?

Only one person can tell us for sure, the resurrected Christ! He might not tell us all we'd like to know, but he tells us all we need to know. He is victor over death. It can claim us only for a season. Our lives, and deaths, are in his hands.

For those who believe, there is only physical death. There is eternal life. But for those who don't believe, there is eternal, spiritual death, separation from God.

Choose life—now and eternally in Jesus Christ. Death

can die for you and all God's promises can come alive if you will turn to the living Lord in faith. What about your faith? Has death died for you? Maybe the Easter reality hasn't come alive for you because you're looking for it in the wrong place.

If you're looking for meaning in life in another person, you won't find it because Christ is the only person to conquer death.

If you're looking for meaning in life in another philosophy, you won't find it because all others are artificial. Christ was God-sent.

If you're looking for meaning in life in the things of this world, you won't find it because the true meaning of life is known only in the resurrected Christ.

"Why do you seek the living among the dead?" The angel's question is still valid. Death died at the resurrection when Christ himself came alive, his words came alive, and his promises came alive. And he can be a living reality in you and become your living Lord. This can be "the day death died" in you, forever! Don't live with the specter of death hanging over you when you can have eternal life. Trust in Jesus Christ as your Savior. Choose him as Lord. Choose life!

15
Can You Believe the Women?
Luke 24:1-11

Patti Wooley has written a marvelous drama entitled, *The Lower Room*. In it she dramatizes what the women who followed Jesus, or who were wives of the apostles, may have been doing downstairs while the men were in the "upper room." When I saw it, I was reminded of a number of things I already knew but needed to rethink.

For one thing, women were historically treated as second-class citizens until Jesus came. Judaism was a male-dominated religion. Women cooked, served, kept the house and children, but did little else. Therefore they were excluded from the "upper room" to the confines of the "lower room."

But it was to women the good news of the resurrection was first announced and to women the risen Lord first appeared. This forever elevated the status of women. They have played a major role in the church from that time. In God's redemptive plan of a new humanity, there is neither "Jew nor Greek, slave nor free, male nor female, for you are all one in Christ Jesus" (Gal. 3:28, NIV).

But at the time and in the setting of the resurrection, that truth wasn't self-evident. The women heard, saw, believed, and obeyed, but there was definitely a question in the disciple's minds, Can we trust the women? There would have been in our minds had we been there.

Mark 16:11 tells us the apostles didn't believe the women. So does Luke 24:11. Look at this in context, Luke 24:1-11.

> But on the first day of the week, at early dawn, they went to the tomb, taking the spices which they had prepared. And they found the stone rolled away from the tomb, but when they went in they did not find the body. While they were perplexed about this, behold two men stood by them in dazzling apparel; and as they were frightened and bowed their faces to the ground, the men said to them, "Why do you seek the living among the dead? Remember how he told you, while he was still in Galilee, that the Son of man must be delivered into the hands of sinful men, and be crucified, and on the third day rise." And they remembered his words, and returning from the tomb they told all this to the eleven and to all the rest. Now it was Mary Magdalene and Joanna and Mary the mother of James and the other women with them who told this to the apostles; but these words seemed to them an idle tale, and they did not believe them.

The disciple's question is our question. Can we believe the women at the empty tomb, that Jesus who died, was crucified, and buried, rose? Can you believe the women?

Yes

The first part of the answer to that question is, Yes, if God's Word means anything. It is the testimony of all four Gospels and every other New Testament book that Jesus rose. This testimony is based on at least twelve post-resurrection appearances. Over five hundred people saw him. It's absolutely amazing that the first of these were women.

Yet, Matthew 28:9 tells us Jesus met the women and spoke to them. Mark 16:9 tells us Jesus appeared first to Mary Magdalene. John 20:18 reports Mary Magdalene telling the disciples, "I have seen the Lord!" These are plain statements of fact we must either accept or reject.

It all comes down to this—the women either saw him and received the message of the resurrection or they were the biggest liars and deceivers who ever lived. Not only so but the veracity, believability, of God's Word is also at stake. If the Bible is true, Jesus rose from the dead and the women can be believed. Otherwise we not only doubt the women but throw the whole Bible away as well. The testimony of the women at the empty tomb and the trustworthiness of the Bible are inexorably bound up into the same tenet of faith.

Can you believe the women? Yes, if God's Word means anything. And it does! It has meant more to people over a longer period of time than any other human writing. Listen to the testimony of some of the world's most renowned leaders about the Bible.

Abraham Lincoln once said, "I believe the Bible is the best gift God has ever given to man. All the good from the Savior of the world is communicated to us through this book."

W. E. Gladstone, the British prime minister and statesman said, "I have known ninety-five of the world's great men in my time, and of those, eighty-seven were followers of the Bible. The Bible is stamped with a specialty of origin, and an immeasurable distance separates it from all competitors."

George Washington asserted, "It is impossible to rightly govern the world without God and the Bible."

Daniel Webster confessed:

> If there is anything in my thoughts or style to commend, the credit is due to my parents for instilling in me an early love of the scriptures. If we abide by the principles taught in the Bible, our country will go on prospering; but if we and our posterity neglect its instructions and authority, no man can tell how sudden a catastrophe may overwhelm us and bury all our glory in profound obscurity.

Patrick Henry, who said "Give me liberty, or give me death!" also said, "The Bible is worth all other books which have ever been printed."

Robert E. Lee testified, "In all my perplexities and distresses, the Bible has never failed to give light and strength."

"It is impossible to enslave mentally or socially a Bible-reading people. The principles of the Bible are the groundwork of human freedom." So stated Horace Greeley, US journalist and politician.

And Charles Dickens wrote, "The New Testament is the very best book that ever was or ever will be known in the world."

Now, stack all these opinions up, consider them carefully and what do we have? Deep faith, tremendous insight, reverence, and respect—yes, but it doesn't equate to the eyewitness accounts of the humble women who were there, who first heard and saw and touched the resurrected Christ.

Yes, you can believe the women at the open tomb because their testimony is true, validated by the total authority and utter believability of God's Holy Word!

Can you believe the women? A part of the answer is yes because God's Word means something.

No

But another part of the answer to the question, Can you believe the women? is, No, unless you experience the resurrected Christ for yourself. Luke 24:10-11 says, "the . . . women . . . told this to the apostles; but these words seemed to them an idle tale, and they did not believe them."

There's no doubt that the women who went to the tomb and found it empty believed what they had seen. It affected the whole course of their lives and ultimately of human history. They had encountered the resurrected Christ and had heard the good news of the angels. "He has risen; he is not here!" They also obeyed the angel's command, "Go, tell his disciples" (Mark 16:6-7). They went, they told, but they were not believed! "These words seemed to them an idle tale."

This says to me that the resurrection, the Easter faith, isn't just intellectual assent to an objective truth. It's not just accepting someone else's word, even if that word is recorded in the Bible. No, the Easter faith is experiencing the resurrected Christ for yourself!

We can't live by someone else's experiences. If your only acquaintance with the resurrected Christ is testimony 2,000 years old, you haven't yet truly experienced him. Jesus didn't just come alive for the people of the Bible. He wants to become a living reality within you. The living Christ only becomes real to you when you commit your life to him.

In *The Lower Room,* Patti Wooley has Mary Magdalene movingly tell of her encounter with the risen Jesus. Then Joanna says, "We must go upstairs and tell the men."

Salome asks, "Will they believe us?"

And Mary Magdalene answers, "Probably not, at first. But he didn't say 'Go convince them.' All he said was, 'Go tell them.'"

It was up to the apostles to experience the resurrected Christ for themselves! They did. They didn't believe the women at first. But there was no denying the reality of their personal encounters with the risen Lord soon after.

And it's up to us to experience the risen Christ ourselves. The same faith is open to you. Have you experienced the living Christ? He becomes real to you when you commit your life to him, not only to know he lives but to say, "he lives within *my* heart."

The testimony of the Bible and of the women at the empty tomb is Jesus lives. Can you believe it? Yes, but only when you've yielded your life to Christ and asked him to become a living reality within you. Have you done that? Do it now!

16
The Emotions of Easter
Luke 24:1-35; John 20:19-20

If you and I had been present the day Christ arose, I wonder what we'd have felt? Whatever our feelings may have been, they'd have been deep. For Easter isn't just a time of faith. It's also a time of feeling. The emotions of Easter run deep, even today. I feel a sense of celebration at Easter. I feel thankful and want to praise. I feel a sense of wonder. I feel keenly the centuries of tradition about this day of days. If we feel all that in the present, we must know that to have been at that first Easter would have brought indescribable feelings. What were the emotions of the first Easter?

What did Mary Magdalene feel at the open tomb, before the angels, when she heard the announcement, when she encountered the Lord in the garden? We know what she saw. What did she feel?

Or the disciples, what were their feelings?

We'd need to read all four of the Gospels to get a full picture of the range of human emotions of that event. Even then, a lot would be left to the imagination. Two of the resurrection narratives present the story in such a way as to enable us to identify at least five emotions of Easter. The first is Luke 24:1-35.

> But on the first day of the week, at early dawn, they went to the tomb, taking the spices which they had prepared. And they found the stone rolled away from the tomb, but when they went in they did not find the body. While they

were perplexed about this, behold, two men stood by them in dazzling apparel; and as they were frightened and bowed their faces to the ground, the men said to them, "Why do you seek the living among the dead? Remember how he told you, while he was still in Galilee, that the Son of man must be delivered into the hands of sinful men, and be crucified, and on the third day rise." And they remembered his words, and returning from the tomb they told all this to the eleven and to all the rest. Now it was Mary Magdalene and Joanna and Mary the mother of James and the other women with them who told this to the apostles; but these words seemed to them an idle tale, and they did not believe them.

That very day two of them were going to a village named Emmaus, about seven miles from Jerusalem, and talking with each other about all these things that had happened. While they were talking and discussing together, Jesus himself drew near and went with them. But their eyes were kept from recognizing him. And he said to them, "What is this conversation which you are holding with each other as you walk?" And they stood still, looking sad. Then one of them, named Cleopas, answered him, "Are you the only visitor to Jerusalem who does not know the things that have happened there in these days?" And he said to him, "What things?" And they said to him, "Concerning Jesus of Nazareth, who was a prophet mighty in deed and word before God and all the people, and how our chief priests and rulers delivered him up to be condemned to death, and crucified him. But we had hoped that he was the one to redeem Israel. Yes, and besides all this, it is now the third day since this happened. Moreover, some women of our company amazed us. They were at the tomb early in the morning and did not find his body; and they came back saying that they had even seen a vision of angels, who said that he was alive. Some of those who were with us went to the tomb, and found it just as the women had said; but him they did not see." And he said to them, "O foolish men, and slow of heart to believe all that the prophets have spoken!

> Was it not necessary that the Christ should suffer these things and enter into his glory?" And beginning with Moses and all the prophets, he interpreted to them in all the scriptures the things concerning himself.
>
> So they drew near to the village to which they were going. He appeared to be going further, but they constrained him, saying, "Stay with us, for it is toward evening and the day is now far spent." So he went in to stay with them. When he was at table with them, he took the bread and blessed, and broke it, and gave it to them. And their eyes were opened and they recognized him; and he vanished out of their sight. They said to each other. "Did not our hearts burn within us while he talked to us on the road, while he opened to us the scriptures?" And they rose that same hour and returned to Jerusalem; and they found the eleven gathered together and those who were with them, who said, "The Lord has risen indeed and has appeared to Simon!" Then they told what had happened on the road, and how he was known to them in the breaking of the bread.

The second is much briefer. It's John 20:19-20.

> On the evening of that day, the first day of the week, the doors being shut where the disciples were, for fear of the Jews, Jesus came and stood among them and said to them, "Peace be with you." When he had said this, he showed them his hands and his side. Then the disciples were glad when they saw the Lord.

We can easily identify at least five feelings, emotions in these verses, felt that first Easter. These emotions are still felt by Easter worshipers everywhere.

Despair

One certain emotion of Easter was the feeling of despair. The disciples felt grief, sadness, gloom, depression. This was a natural feeling. They'd lost their leader on whom they'd pinned all their hopes. We can feel their despair going to the tomb, the heaviness of their hearts in their saddening task. We can feel it at the tomb, when they didn't find the body of their beloved. We can feel it back at headquarters, deep within the hearts of the waiting disciples.

Luke 24:17 speaks of the disciples on the Emmaus road "looking sad." We can hear their despair in verse 21, "But we had hoped that he was the one to redeem Israel." There's no doubt they were on bottom! Despair was a major emotion that Easter.

How do you handle despair? How do you overcome it? Much has been written on this subject in recent years. There seems to be some concensus of general principles or steps to take to rise out of despair.

First, you must acknowledge the fact. There's no hope of overcoming depression without the recognition that you're down. Don't be ashamed. Admit you're depressed. It's the first step on the road back.

Then try to determine the cause. What's getting you down? There are many possible causes—feelings of rejection, helplessness, sin, guilt, low self-esteem. There are sometimes physical reasons—hormonal imbalance, nutrition, overweight. And there are many combinations of these causes in addition to many others. What's bugging you? Try to find out.

There will always be alternatives you can choose which will bring relief. For instance, if sin is the problem, maybe confession is the solution. Or maybe you just need to get a different perspective on your problem or on yourself. Perhaps if you helped someone else with a problem, it would help you get a handle on your own. There are many alternatives to consider.

Turn to God for help. He's always there. He cares. Think about God. Fix your mind on his presence and love. Read your Bible and helpful Christian literature. There's a wealth of help available in print. Pray. Nothing beats it for spiritual aid and insight. Nothing even comes close.

Consider contacting a "helper" to aid you in dealing with your problem. This may be a counselor, doctor, pastor, friend, family member. Anyone skilled and caring might be able to help. Don't be afraid to seek help when you need it.

The disciples didn't despair long, and neither should we. God will help you in dealing with despair. The gospel of Jesus is good news to cheer the breaking heart!

Fear

Fear was an emotion of Easter. "They were frightened," Luke says of the women at the open tomb. The angels scared the daylights out of them.

Meanwhile, the disciples were huddled behind locked doors in the upper room "for fear of the Jews." They had good reason to fear. Their lives were in jeopardy. Their fear was real and natural.

We're kindred here! We fear all kinds of things, feelings, and even other people. We fear everything from failure to too much success, from death to living with pain, from public speaking to private intimacy.

I can easily remember my most frightening experience. My son was just a few months old and couldn't yet walk. But, boy could he crawl! My wife and I were going out, and she was ready first. She offered to go get the baby sitter, and I let her.

Brian, our son, was playing on the bathroom floor while I shaved and dressed in the upstairs bathroom. I just took my eyes off him for a second. But when I looked back, he was gone. Then, thumpity-bump-bump, I heard him fall down the stairs. I rushed to the head of the stairs to look down on his little body at the foot, on the tile floor, perfectly still. I thought he was dead.

Well, by the time I descended those sixteen steps in two bounds, he was screaming his head off, much to my relief! He cried and I comforted, and I don't know which of us was more frightened. But he was OK, and after a while, so was I.

Fear is a natural response to many situations, sometimes justified, sometimes not. Fear can be overcome by faith. We must face our fears with courage and conviction to conquer them. Otherwise, they'll control us. Jesus often said, "Fear not!" We must take his advice to heart.

Doubt

Doubt was deep in the emotions of the first Easter. At the tomb doubt was the first feeling, soon overcome by the angel's annunciation. When the women reported what they'd seen and heard, the disciples doubted them. On the Emmaus road, doubt played a role in the inability to see Jesus as himself. Thomas doubted. Boy, did Thomas doubt! And he kept on until he saw and experienced the risen Christ for himself.

Doubt isn't all bad. It sometimes leads to great discoveries and new truth. Witness Thomas. It's only bad when you doubt without making any effort to overcome it. To have doubts is normal. But to live in doubt is debilitating.

We overcome doubt by self-searching to satisfactory certainty. Don't camp under the tent of doubt. Doubt your doubts until you discover the truth that sets you free!

Amazement

Surely one of the emotions of Easter was amazement, wonder, awe. The women at the tomb were awe-struck by the angels. Wouldn't you have been? Wonder and amazement filled the air in the upper room at the appearances of

Jesus. The disciples on the Emmaus road were amazed to find out it was the Lord!

Anyone who considers the resurrection, then or now, is naturally filled with amazement. The resurrection is so mind-boggling as to stupefy the most sedate. We come to the tomb in wonder and leave with a holy shock. Jesus, who was crucified, lives! Let every knee bend in wonder and every head bow in awe!

Joy

Unbridled joy is the final emotion of Easter. The Emmaus road disciples were so joy-filled they went all the way back to Jerusalem and exclaimed, "The Lord has risen indeed!" That's joy!

John says, "Then the disciples were glad when they saw the Lord." This was their final feeling, and the most important. Those present at the first Easter worked through all their other feelings to the joy.

This is where Easter leads us! We don't stop on the dead-end street of despair. We can't fret in the fetters of fear. We mustn't dwell in a dungeon of doubt. We shouldn't intoxicate ourselves in the thin air of amazement. We must let Easter lead us to the unbridled joy which is the outcome of true Easter faith!

Easter feelings still run deep. The whole range of human emotions are capsulized in the experience of this event. Don't park by the inferior feelings. Move to joy, celebration, praise, life. These are the nobler emotions of Easter. Because Jesus lives we can know life!

Section III

Were You There . . . After the Resurrection?

17
The Cover-Up
Matthew 28:11-15

The world was shocked when it learned that the then President of the United States, Richard M. Nixon, had on March 22, 1973 told his closest associates—H. R. Haldeman, John Ehrlichman, John Mitchell, and John Dean—to cover up information about the break-in at the Democratic National Headquarters at the Watergate. "Stonewall it" were Nixon's exact words, meaning they were to suppress information from the Senate investigating committee.

Eventually Richard Nixon resigned in disgrace. Each of the others involved in the cover-up, along with other high government officials, were convicted of conspiracy to obstruct justice or other high crimes. Watergate was a sad chapter in American history.

But there is in Scripture another cover-up so serious it would make Watergate look like a game at a Sunday School picnic. It was the attempted cover-up of the reality of the resurrection by the Jewish authorities, recorded in Matthew 28:11-15.

Jesus had risen from the grave. Roman guards at the tomb were eyewitnesses to all that went on. They may have seen the angels descending, the stone rolled away, the risen Christ emerge, the arrival of the women. Perhaps they even overheard Jesus tell the women to go tell his disciples to meet him in Galilee. Then, we read in Matthew 28:11-15,

> While they were going, behold, some of the guard went into the city and told the chief priests all that had taken

> place. And when they had assembled with the elders and taken counsel, they gave a sum of money to the soldiers and said, "Tell people 'His disciples came by night and stole him away while we were asleep.' And if this comes to the governor's ears, we will satisfy him and keep you out of trouble." So they took the money and did as they were directed; and this story has been spread among the Jews to this day.

"The cover-up," or, maybe we should call it "Golgotha-gate." Never has there been a deed so dastardly or a lie so brazen as the conspiracy to cover up the resurrection of Jesus.

Had we been there, would we have been party to it? Let's examine this act and learn from it so we may never be party to denying the living Lord. There are three powerful lessons in "the cover-up."

Willful Sin

Willful sin occasions a cover-up. The conspiracy to cover up the resurrection was consciously chosen. They deliberately chose to deny Christ. The Jewish leaders knew Jesus had said he'd rise on the third day (Matt. 27:63). They had eyewitness accounts this had come true. They should have fallen on their faces and confessed Jesus as Lord! Instead, they conspired together and initiated a cover-up. It was a willful, deliberate sin, the result of unbelief.

Some people will never believe. Those Jewish authorities knew Jesus was alive again. But they chose to cover it up and lie about it. There was no doubt the tomb was empty. The Romans, Jews, and Christians all acknowledged that fact. It was a matter of faith and commitment to the truth that made the difference. The cover-up was a result of a willful denial of the risen Christ. There was ample evidence of the resurrection. But they chose not to believe, choosing rather to cover up the truth with lies. That's as willful and blatant a sin as has ever been committed.

I remember a drama about a group of people who lived in a huge, dark, dank barn. These people worshiped the sun. The only problem was, they lived in darkness. No one had seen the sun for many, many years. They lived in the center of the barn and no one was allowed to go near the outer walls.

One day an outsider came into the barn. He told the barn people the sun they worshiped was real. He'd seen it. He told them he could lead them out of their darkness into the sun's true light. The young people were captivated by what he said. The older people, especially the religious establishment, resisted.

Finally the rebel got a group to follow him outside the barn. There they saw the sun and felt its warmth. Later they returned to the barn and said, "We saw the true sun." But the group that remained in the barn said, "No, we are the true sun worshipers!"

There's an old adage that says, "There are none so blind as those who will not see."

No multiplication of evidence can convince those who stubbornly refuse to believe the truth. Jesus is alive! But unless that becomes a life-altering statement of faith for you, personally, then he might as well not be alive. To choose to believe is salvation. But to be exposed to the truth and choose not to believe is sin. The choice is up to you.

Chain Reaction

Covering up sin is a chain-reaction process. The Jews involved in the cover-up of Jesus' resurrection rediscovered an old spiritual principle: "One sin leads to another."

Their cover-up was a chain reaction process. It began with the bribe. They bribed the guards. Then they got to thinking, *What if Pilate hears about it?* They conspired to bribe the governor! "We will satisfy him."

The lie was also a chain-reaction process. It began with them lying to themselves by denial. Then they bribed the guards to perpetuate the lie, and the lie spread. Matthew says, "and this story has been spread among the Jews to this day."

Sin compounds itself. Those involved in this conspiracy not only chose not to believe for themselves but also they took it upon themselves to keep others from believing! This is compounded sin—one sin drawing on another, "iniquity upon iniquity."

There was a potato chip commercial on television where one person offers a chip to another and says "Betcha can't eat one." The person takes a chip, then wants another. "Uh, uh," says the offerer, "I said *one*." The point is, those chips are so good nobody can eat just one.

The same principle applies to sin. One sin leads to another and another. It's a chain-reaction process!

The sin process stops with faith in Jesus Christ. He brings forgiveness. Instead of multiplied sin we experience multiplied grace, each sin leading to forgiveness. But it's up to you to confess your sin rather than covering it up. When you confess, forgiveness is yours by faith.

Truth Will Out

Ultimately the truth can't be covered up. All of the efforts of the Jewish cover-up of the resurrection were for naught. Sealing the stone, placing the guards on twenty-four-hour watch, even the conspiracy, the bribes, and the lies all serve to reinforce the truth that Jesus rose!

History and experience have proven the reality of the resurrection. The truth will out!

In time the attempted cover-up was shown for what it was—willful sin. Sin always surfaces. Numbers 32:23 says, "Be sure your sin will find you out." And even if you could cover up your sin for all your life and keep it from every other person, someday you'll stand before God and he knows you—every sin, every thought, and every action. Sin always surfaces.

But truth will triumph. There's no untruth so pervasive as to ultimately cover the truth. No conspiracy can contain Christ. If the grave couldn't, people's lies sure can't. He lives! And in each generation many have experienced him as the true and living way. Truth outlives falsehood, outshines darkness, and exposes evil. That's always true and ever shall be. The truth can't be covered up!

As we look at ourselves, perhaps we take pride in the fact we've never covered up the reality of the resurrection. But the truth is, we have. We cover up the resurrection every time we willfully sin, every time we act or speak or live as if Christ weren't alive.

Willful sin causes a cover-up. It's a chain-reaction process. The truth can't be covered up. And the truth is, Jesus who died lives again and wants to live in you. He can by your faith!

18
What Do We Do After Easter?
Matthew 28:16-20

The resurrection of Jesus is the single most important event in the Christian faith. It confirmed everything the Old Testament taught and everything Jesus did and said up to the cross. It assured all God's promises from the cross onward. Had we been present on the first Easter no doubt we'd have entered into the significance of the event with full faith and wonder.

But what do you do after Easter? I mean, everything pivots on the resurrection. What next is of significance?

If you were a Jewish leader or Roman authority of the first century, you might have joined in the attempt to cover up the news of the resurrection. But as a follower of Jesus Christ, you would have fallen under the risen Lord's command to carry out his work in the world.

This is the teaching of Matthew 28:16-20. It's one of the most significant passages in the Bible. Known as the "Great Commission," in these verses Jesus commanded his followers to carry out his work in the world. We are his followers, therefore we are to fulfill the Great Commission of Jesus Christ. Hear his orders for what we're to do after Easter.

> Now the eleven disciples went to Galilee, to the mountain to which Jesus had directed them. And when they saw him they worshiped him; but some doubted. And Jesus came and said to them, "All authority in heaven and on earth has been given to me. Go therefore and make disciples of all

nations, baptizing them in the name of the Father and of the Son and of the Holy Spirit, teaching them to observe all that I have commanded you; and lo, I am with you always, to the close of the age."

These are familiar words to followers of Jesus. We've heard many stirring missions messages preached from this text. Much emphasis is usually placed on the word *go*. But a careful examination of the word translated *go* reveals it's not an imperative verb but a participle best translated "as you go" or "while going." Jesus confidently expected his disciples to go into all the world. His command was to "make disciples" as they went. Their task was to carry on his work. That's what they were to do after Easter.

This is our task. As we go about our normal affairs of life, we are to make disciples along the way. That's what we're to do in light of the open tomb and in the power of the resurrected Christ. This is an important task. As we do it, we must remember three things from Jesus' words in the Great Commission.

Can't Do It Alone

First, we can't do it alone. The task of discipling the nations is too big for mere human efforts. The unreached multitudes are too numerous. Without help, it's impossible to carry out the great post-Easter commission.

The good news is we don't have to do it alone! We can do it in the power of the risen Christ. Jesus said, "all authority in heaven and on earth has been given to me." He has the power to enable us to get his work done. And he added, "I am with you always." You can't beat that! The very power and presence of Christ is promised to those who attempt to carry out his commands. We are to appropriate the power and acknowledge the presence as we go. It's available for the asking. We don't have to go it alone!

There's an old story about a custodian at Spurgeon's

Tabernacle in London showing some visitors around the famous church. As he guided them, he asked if they'd like to see the power room. Assuming he meant a room where all kinds of electrical and mechanical equipment operated, the tourists weren't too excited. But out of courtesy they agreed.

The custodian led them down a long corridor with a single door at the end. He quietly opened the door. The visitors were amazed to see inside a roomful of people praying! They prayed for their pastor, the sick, the lost, for salvation, and for the whole world. Truly this was the power center of this great church!

Jesus Christ makes his power available to us for the asking. We can't win the whole world alone. But we don't have to. Jesus' power and presence is with us. Therefore we can accomplish the task he's commanded us to do. He never issues an order without the offer of assistance for its accomplishment. Appropriate the power and acknowledge the presence!

Can't Do It Easily

As we try to obey Jesus' after-Easter order, we come to realize we can't do it easily. In fact, carrying out God's work in the world is the most difficult task ever ordered. When Jesus did it, it cost him his life. Now, after Easter, he says we are to do it. What a task! It isn't easy.

The difficult assignment he gave us is twofold. First, it's evangelistic. We're to "make disciples of all nations, baptizing them in the name of the Father and of the Son and of the Holy Spirit." That's a tall order! But evangelization is the primary task of the church. We're to do many things in Jesus' name. But first and foremost is to gather in disciples by conversion. We're to lead people to a saving knowledge of Jesus Christ, and that's never easy. But you know what? It's not supposed to be! Jesus never promised us ease, only power and presence. He said he'd be with us, in us, to do the work. We must set our hearts on the work of winning the world to Christ. Not easy. Just possible.

The second part of our assignment is discipling those who are won. "Teaching them to observe all that I have commanded you," is the way Jesus put it. After they're won, they must be taught. Who's to do that but you and me? No one! So our task is to develop disciples as Jesus did. This won't be done easily. It will take dedication and persistence. But, with Jesus' power and presence it can be done.

During World War II, Winston Churchill was the inspiration behind many people and victories. When all of Europe was lost to Hitler except England, and it looked as if she too would topple, Churchill rallied his people by pointing out that he had "nothing to offer but blood, toil, tears and sweat." But with bulldog tenacity, he offered all he and his people had against the Nazi tyranny. He exclaimed, "we'll fight them in the air, we'll fight them in the sea, we'll fight them on the land—on our shores, in our cities, in our homes." And fight they did, to victory. Why? Because they were committed to do the difficult.

The task of carrying on Christ's work in the world is difficult. But it's necessary. The lost must be told of Jesus. Those won to faith must be taught. Ours is this task. We must dedicate ourselves totally to God and toil on.

Can't Do It Quickly

The farther we get from the original Easter the more obvious it becomes we can't carry out Christ's command quickly. Jesus indicated the ongoing nature of his work in the world when he promised his power and presence "to the close of the age." This is a reference to the consummation of the world at Christ's second coming.

Christians since Jesus' time have been working. Ours is

no quick and easy task. We're working within the limitations of time and space. We're limited by our own finiteness. But these are no excuses to avoid or delay working for Christ. We're to be about our Father's business. Jesus is coming again. We look forward to that glorious prospect with eager expectation. But we must toil on until that day.

All worthwhile things take time. It takes nine months to have a baby. A college degree usually requires four years of study. It takes years to master an art, craft, or occupation. William Carey spent seven long years in India before he baptized the first convert.

We can't win the world to Christ in a day. He couldn't. Neither can we. But we can't stop trying. We must "work, for the night is coming." Keep on. Time is on our side. Don't quit when everything doesn't change overnight. Work on in the power and presence of Christ. He hasn't rescinded his orders and the Great Commission hasn't been completely fulfilled yet. So we're to work on until he comes or calls us to his side.

What do we do after Easter? The Great Commission challenges us to carry on Christ's work in the world. We can't do it alone. It isn't easy. It won't be done quickly. But with Christ's power and presence, we can do it. We simply must dedicate ourselves totally to the task.

How about it?